my GRIEF HANDBOOK

WHY GRIEF HURTS AND HOW TO COPE

DAVID TRICKEY, BECK FERRARI *and* OLIVIA CLARK-TATE

ILLUSTRATED BY ROBERTA RAVASIO

Jessica Kingsley Publishers
London and Philadelphia

First published in Great Britain in 2024 by Jessica Kingsley Publishers
An imprint of John Murray Press

1

Printed and bound in Great Britain by TJ Books Ltd

Jessica Kingsley Publishers' policy is to use papers that are natural,
renewable and recyclable products and made from wood grown in
sustainable forests. The logging and manufacturing processes are expected
to conform to the environmental regulations of the country of origin.

Jessica Kingsley Publishers
Carmelite House
50 Victoria Embankment
London EC4Y 0DZ

www.jkp.com

John Murray Press
Part of Hodder & Stoughton Limited
An Hachette UK Company

For Donna

CONTENTS

ACKNOWLEDGEMENTS

Thank you to all the young people and families we have worked with. You have shared your stories, your problems and your concerns with us. And you have taught us so much about what helps and what people are capable of; you are truly inspiring.

We'd also like to thank our own families, friends and colleagues who have supported us, particularly our children.

PREFACE

We're sorry you're having to read this book, because it probably means someone important in your life has died. Whenever and however that happened, it will most likely be tough and will hurt. We hope this book can be some kind of navigation tool to help you find your way in your grief. When we say a 'navigation tool', we need to explain that this is no Google Maps with a fast-route and a short-route option. But we hope to help you make sense of the landscape you are experiencing and give you some ideas that help you cope with whatever direction your grief is taking you.

If you're an adult of a bereaved teenager reading this book to help you understand more about grief, then good on you. If you're the friend of a teenager who is grieving, then that's great that you're being such a good friend and wanting to understand a bit more about what your friend is going through and how you can support them.

How can this book help?

Lots of people talk about needing to 'process' grief. Even though we sometimes use this word, we still wonder what it actually means! We hope that spending time thinking through and making sense of what hurts and why, and then finding your ways to cope are all tasks that can help with 'processing'.

There's no wrong way to do grief, and there's no one-size-fits-all solution in terms of support. Sometimes the reactions of adults and others around you can make you feel that you are 'doing your grief wrong'. They might suggest you need to see an expert such as a counsellor or therapist. That might be really helpful if your grief is extra heavy, and you feel you need help to manage it. But there is no automatic need for specialist psychological help. And with support from home, friends and school, many young people find a way to do their grief and adjust to life. Many bereaved teenagers also find it helpful to connect with others who are bereaved within a group or have some 1:1 time to talk to someone.

This book will give you some ideas to help you work out how you are getting on and whether any of our suggestions make a difference to how you are coping. You can then talk it through with an adult you trust, to help you work out whether you could do with some more help. There are some ideas for when and where to get more help in Chapter 3.

As well as giving you our ideas from working with and learning from many, many bereaved young people, Olivia, our amazing young-person co-author, has been working to help keep us in check. Olivia's dad died when she was a teenager. As our expert by experience, Olivia has helped make sure that we are speaking about young people's experiences of grief in a way that seems accurate and respectful. And she has added some personal experiences of her own, too.

We have also included some characters to help explain and give examples of what we mean. None of these characters are real individuals, but their stories have been created using a mixture of the stories of young people we have supported.

OLIVIA'S PERSONAL EXPERIENCE

Grief is very lonely at times, and sometimes being a teenager sucks, too! You're learning how to grow up and navigating such a confusing world of emotions and physical changes that it's easy to get overwhelmed without realizing. This overwhelming feeling can be scary and make you think you can't talk to people. But find people you trust and tell them how you're feeling.

Your emotions can feel so scrambled that your judgement may not be as good as you think, and if you're worried that you might do something silly and dangerous, tell someone you trust. Grief is weird, and it can make us want to do things we might not have wanted to do before, because our minds are looking for outlets for our thoughts and emotions, but trust your gut; if you don't like how you're feeling, or you don't understand some of your emotions/thoughts/decisions, reach out to someone you trust. Try new ways to cope with your grief, but keeping yourself safe is so important, and it can be easy to overlook and lose sight of that.

All pages marked ⊕ can be downloaded from https://library.jkp.com/redeem using the code QHVZEQJ

Chapter 1

WHY BEREAVEMENT IS SO HARD

Grief is the price we pay for love

What probably makes bereavement so tough is experiencing the permanent loss of someone important, and still having to somehow get on with everything that everyone expects you to be doing at this time in your life. The phrase 'grief is the price we pay for love'[1] goes some way towards helping to explain this. Because the person who died was significant to you, and you had an important relationship with them, it is probably going to hurt a lot when they are no longer there.

Psychologists describe strong relationships as attachments. These are the bonds of warmth, love and security that we have with key people – often our family or close friends. In spite of daily ups and downs, these relationships are seen to be the foundation of wellbeing and good development.

---

1 Parkes, C.M. (1972) *Bereavement: Studies of Grief in Adult Life.* London: Tavistock.

So it's inevitable that it's going to hurt a lot when that person is gone and you can no longer have them physically in your life.

While attachment may mean the pain you feel at their death is at times overwhelming, it is this same foundation of love that gives you something powerful to hold on to, knowing how special that person was to you and you were to them.

But grief is individual, and the depth of your grief is not related to how much you loved the person or how good your relationship was. Sometimes even though you loved the person who has died very much, your pain can feel more manageable, and you may have all sorts of reasons for not finding grief so very hard. Sometimes, the relationship you had with the person who died was complicated, or perhaps they were already absent in your life, and yet you find that after their death, it is a real (and understandable) struggle to manage your grief (more about this in Chapter 2). Sometimes we grieve for the love we *should* have had and maybe one day hoped to have, and that can really, really hurt.

As we were saying above, our experiences of having strong bonds can give us strength to draw on while grieving. It's as though these relationships give us strong roots to help us weather the storm of the grief and the tornado of feelings it can bring. Grief can blow us around a lot and leave us feeling pretty *battered*, but somehow our roots keep us secure. Those roots that are going to support you might be based on strong relationships you've had in the past that have given you a certain sense of feeling secure which will now help you weather the storm.

But your roots might also be formed of ongoing current relationships (with friends, family and furry friends) and the support that they can give you. The roots may even be based on an ongoing connection with the person who has died – even if that seems weird. But lots of people continue to have a relationship of some sort with someone who has died.

Of course, it's a different relationship to the one they had when the person was alive, but it's still a relationship – the person who died can continue to play a part in your life.

You may not have had so many strong relationships in your growing-up years, so when someone dies, that brings even more challenges and another hard thing to manage on top of the pain you may have been through. On the other hand, often this gives you lots of experience in being blown around by the storms of life. And you might be able to use what you have learned from these other storms to help you get through each day with your grief. Maybe the friendships and relationships in your life right now are not really the most steady or helpful and that makes coping a bit harder. But this book is full of ideas to help you cope, and they don't all rely on someone else.

You are probably finding out about the price of your grief with the many different ways the death of someone important has affected you. Young people we have worked with have told us about the different ways their grief costs them: the physical cost, the emotional cost, the thinking cost and the practical cost.

Physical: the way your grief is affecting your body

Feelings are not just in your mind – they affect your body, too. You may be feeling a lot more tired, and yet, unhelpfully, less able to sleep deeply. You may feel like your body still feels a bit shocked by the news – this can come back to you even some time after the first shock has passed. After an earthquake, there can still be really big 'aftershocks' for quite a while after. Even when your mind is busy with something else, you can feel as if your body is still carrying around a big weight of grief right inside your chest, a kind of heaviness in your heart. You might feel generally unwell or have specific aches and pains associated with the deep pain of your grief. If you are worried about the way your body is feeling, tell an adult and get your GP to check.

66 I just don't have the energy for anything – I'm so tired. (Tara)

66 Even though I had a good time with my friends tonight, my chest just feels so heavy. (Kareem)

66 I keep getting a stomach ache; it's probably nothing, but I don't feel hungry any more. (Jared)

Emotional: the way your grief is affecting how you feel

There is no official list of feelings that go with grief – what you're feeling is what you're feeling! You might have all sorts of shocked, sad, angry, worried, lonely feelings. You might also have some comforting ones about feeling loved, happy, peaceful or relieved. It's your grief – and you won't find us telling you that you're feeling the 'wrong' thing!

Each feeling that you have may differ in how big or strong it feels. One day your cross feelings can feel small enough to manage, but the next day they feel big and get in the way of everything. And then the next day they aren't there at all. You may experience any number of feelings in any one day – you might find that your feelings change rapidly, catch you out when you aren't expecting them, or you might find that you feel stuck feeling the same way for a long time. Perhaps you find that you are holding on to opposite feelings at the same time – this can be hard to get your head around, and it doesn't seem to make sense.

> **“** I'm really sad that Dad isn't here to watch this movie with me. And I even miss him trying to take handfuls of my popcorn. But when I watch it, I also get some comfort and happiness from the memory of laughing with Dad when we saw it before. (Tara)

Thinking: the way your grief affects how and what you think

Lots of young people tell us that concentrating on things is really hard when someone has died, especially at first. Keeping your attention on one thing can be difficult – sometimes because thoughts about the person who died or thoughts about your grief can keep popping into your mind, and other times because people's minds just wander. Sometimes thinking about what happened to the person who died can take up a lot of room in your mind, making it hard to listen and remember what other people are saying. Sometimes because it is so hard to think what happened, you might try really hard NOT to think about it.

Our brains are really annoying, though, and the thing we're trying not to think about usually keeps coming back anyway. Psychologists call this *ironic rebound*. It's a bit like when you have a really annoying song going around in your head, and the more you try to *stop* thinking about it, the more it goes round and round. This can be particularly true for 'traumatic deaths', which we talk about more later.

Your grief can also affect *what* you think, and you might find that you are thinking about things differently. It can change how you think about yourself, your life, others around you and the world in general.

66 I keep thinking, why did it have to happen to me and my family? (Emily)

66 I've always looked after my little sister – now that she has died, I'm not sure who I am any more. (Amara)

66 Now I think I want to be a chef like my mum – that would make her really proud. (Liam)

66 I keep thinking that everyone else is going to leave me like my friend did – it's hard to trust people now. (Simran)

Practical: the way your grief affects everyday life

Life might have changed quite a lot for you since your person died – in fact, it might have changed massively for you. Not only are your body, your feelings and your mind trying to adjust to these changes, but there may be lots of practical changes for you. And changes can feel hard, especially when you didn't necessarily choose the changes. These changes can be in everyday things, such as who gets the dinner, who drops you at swimming club or where you go at the weekend. But sometimes after someone has died it's possible that there are massive changes in where you live, who you live with and where you go to school. That can be a lot to cope with on top of all the other grieving stuff.

66 Morning isn't the same now as I don't get the bus with my brother. (Lara)

66 I can't get to swimming club any more as my dad now works in the evenings. (Dylan)

66 Bedtime feels really different as I can't text my boyfriend to say 'Goodnight'. (Maryam)

66 I don't miss going to the nursing home every weekend, but it is kind of empty not visiting Nan any more. (Carlos)

We've drawn up lists of some of the ways your grief might be costing you. Have a read through and, thinking about the last two weeks, fill in whether each one is **not at all**, **a bit** or **a lot**. There's no fancy system to total up the price of your grief, but it could help you understand what the cost is for you. And we hope you can then give yourself a thumbs up because you're managing all of that. These lists are repeated at the back of the book.

THE PHYSICAL COST

	Not at all	A bit	A lot
I am more tired	☐	☐	☐
It's hard to get to sleep or stay asleep	☐	☐	☐
I haven't got much energy	☐	☐	☐
My body feels in shock	☐	☐	☐
My body feels heavy and sluggish	☐	☐	☐
My chest (or heart) feels heavy	☐	☐	☐
My body feels restless so it's hard to relax	☐	☐	☐
My throat feels tight or as though there's a knot in it	☐	☐	☐
My eyes feel like they could cry at any moment	☐	☐	☐
My head is a bit foggy and confused	☐	☐	☐
My stomach has a knot in it or just won't settle	☐	☐	☐
It is harder to eat	☐	☐	☐
I keep wanting to eat	☐	☐	☐
(Write in your own)	☐	☐	☐
. . . .			
(Write in your own)	☐	☐	☐
. . . .			

THE EMOTIONAL COST

	Not at all	A bit	A lot
I feel sad or upset	☐	☐	☐
I feel worried or scared	☐	☐	☐
I feel cross or annoyed	☐	☐	☐
I feel guilty or ashamed	☐	☐	☐
I feel lonely	☐	☐	☐
I feel heartbroken	☐	☐	☐
My feelings change a lot	☐	☐	☐
My feelings get in the way of doing stuff	☐	☐	☐
I get opposite feelings that are tricky to manage (e.g. sad and happy at the same time)	☐	☐	☐
My feelings are so big that they overwhelm me	☐	☐	☐
(Write in your own)	☐	☐	☐
. . . .			
(Write in your own)	☐	☐	☐
. . . .			

THE THINKING COST

	Not at all	A bit	A lot
It's hard to concentrate	☐	☐	☐
I keep forgetting things	☐	☐	☐
I feel like I'm in a fog	☐	☐	☐
My mind keeps thinking about what happened	☐	☐	☐
I keep trying to make sense of something that doesn't really make sense	☐	☐	☐
I spend a lot of time trying NOT to think about what happened	☐	☐	☐
I'm thinking about me and my life in an unhelpful way	☐	☐	☐
I'm thinking about other people in an unhelpful way	☐	☐	☐
I'm thinking about the world around me in an unhelpful way	☐	☐	☐
(Write in your own)	☐	☐	☐
. . . .			
(Write in your own)	☐	☐	☐
. . . .			

THE PRACTICAL COST

	Not at all	A bit	A lot
My morning has changed	☐	☐	☐
My daytime has changed	☐	☐	☐
My evening has changed	☐	☐	☐
My weekends have changed	☐	☐	☐
Who I get to see has changed	☐	☐	☐
Who I live with has changed	☐	☐	☐
Where I go to school has changed	☐	☐	☐
Things I used to enjoy have stopped	☐	☐	☐
My responsibilities have changed	☐	☐	☐
The people I used to rely on have changed	☐	☐	☐
(Write in your own)	☐	☐	☐

. . . .

(Write in your own)	☐	☐	☐

. . . .

Remember, these lists don't give you a *score* to show you how costly your grief is, but they will help you give yourself some credit for everything you are managing right now. You might want to come back to this list and fill it in again in a few months to see how things are going and if they seem to be getting a bit better, a bit worse, or staying the same. If things seem to be getting worse, then it would be worth thinking about finding some extra support. We've put some ideas in Chapter 3.

The cost of grief can also be heavy because it's not just about what's happening today. It's about the past, the present and the future. You might feel as though you are carrying around the memories from yesterday, trying to cope with feelings of today and then working to get your head around a future that won't be the same.

We're all different

We mentioned earlier about this book being a bit like a sat nav, giving you some ideas about navigating your grief. Although we hope that some of the book helps, we can't plot an exact route for you – the path you take will be individual to you. We can't tell you the 'right' or 'wrong' way to do your grief, but we can help you find ways to negotiate some of the challenges as you find your way.

OLIVIA'S PERSONAL EXPERIENCE

For me, grief has been an interesting process of going back and forth on my emotions. And eight years later, I have had days harder than right after I experienced the loss. I think it's something that will always be with me. I lost my dad when I was 13, and that's such a challenging age as it is with puberty, emotions and school among other things. While I was figuring out who I was as a person, and shaping into a young adult, I was also now navigating a bereavement that was going to shape me and permanently change my emotions and memories. The best advice I can offer – don't overthink it and don't try to force your grief to be 'completed' in X amount of time. You have to ride this wave and allow yourself to feel your grief fully.

What makes your grief individual to you is what you bring to your grief and how this shapes how you see and experience the world. This is influenced by many things, including your identity and character, people around you, your beliefs, the things that have happened in your past and how life is now. Being neurodiverse or neurotypical, being straight, gay, trans, having a disability, being care experienced, being from a particular ethnic background, or having a religion or faith that plays an important role in your life – these will all have an impact on the way you make sense of what has happened and therefore how you do your grief. We hope that some of what we describe in this book makes sense to you and helps you find ways to grieve that feel supportive of you as an individual.

Inside grief, outside grief

How you feel your grief on the inside and how you express your grief on the outside are also different for everyone. Others around you may have views on how you should grieve. You may (or may not) find it helpful when they tell you about them!

Often people say, 'I know exactly how you feel.' The chances are, they probably don't!

They might know a bit – but probably not exactly how you feel. Does that mean that your grief is entirely unique? Maybe, but it's more likely that what you feel and when and how you feel it are individual to you. And the *what* and *when* and *how* you express your grief are personal to you, too.

OLIVIA'S PERSONAL EXPERIENCE

People would tell me they knew how I felt because they were letting me know they cared, but being sad, angry (all of the emotions!), it just pushed me inside my own head more at times. You might feel isolated and like no one really gets you. And most people won't get exactly how you're feeling – how can they?! But I found it helpful to let my friends and family know when I was having sadder days or happier days, so that they understood where I was at with my grief for that day. It was easier for me, letting my friends know I was sad that day before someone, without trying to be mean, made a comment saying how grumpy or tired I looked. Those sorts of comments used to push me back inside my own head more, and it made me want to share less with people how I was feeling. Your grief is unique and personal, and no one but you knows what is going on inside your head, but you can let those you trust know as much as you want about how you feel so you can understand it together.

Psychologists suggest that when we are grieving, we need to 'feel the feelings' – that is, to recognize and experience the emotions of our grief. This can be hard when what we are feeling seems so big that we'd like to hide from the feelings and pretend they don't exist. Feeling the feelings doesn't mean that we need to feel them and live with them all the time.

It can take a lot of strength to get on with each day when you are grieving. Maybe you feel that you can leave it behind to some extent while you are busy at school, or maybe it feels as though it goes with you wherever you are. In order to be able to face people and do stuff, you might find that you put on your 'outside' or 'public' face.

Public vs private

It can be useful to work out which emotions you show in public and which you tend to keep more private.

Is there a big difference between public you and private you?

Who gets to see private you?

Private you   **Public you**

There can be an upside and a downside to both public
and private emotions. Young people have told us about the
upsides and downsides to the way they do their grief:

	Public emotions	Private emotions
Upside	People have a good idea about what I'm feeling and can support me.	It can be easier to get on with my day.
	I am being 'true' to myself.	I feel more protected from other people's view of me.
Downside	It can be hard to get on with my day if I am 'wearing' my grief.	People have no idea what I'm feeling so find it hard to support me.
	I can feel exposed and judged by others.	It can feel exhausting to have to carry around so much hidden grief.

What are the upsides and downsides for you?

	Public emotions	Private emotions
Upside		
Downside		

When we hide a lot of our grief, those around us can struggle to understand how we are doing and find it hard to support us in the way we need.

We might also be hiding our feelings from ourselves. Sometimes this is what we need to get through something important in the short term. In the long term, though, if we are going to be able to adapt and learn to live with our grief, we will need to face and feel our feelings.

Does the way you are sharing and hiding your feelings work for you?

Is there anything you could try differently?

Sometimes even the feelings we show in public can be misinterpreted by those around us. For example, sometimes people think we are being moody when in fact we feel down or upset. Or maybe we are showing angry but really we are feeling hurt.

Can you think of a time when your feelings have been misunderstood? What happened as a result?

Sometimes to be understood we need to more than simply show – we may also need to tell someone.

Who can you tell? Is there someone at home? School? A friend? A trusted adult?

Comparing our grief

Sometimes people try to 'measure' their grief, as if it were something that could be measured with a ruler. Sometimes other people around you say things about how bad it is for others.

66 At least you got to have your dad around for 14 years – your little sister will barely remember him. (Jared)

This doesn't usually make you feel any better. The only person you can really compare your grief with is yourself. Is this the worst thing you have had to face? If so, that's really tough, so go easy on yourself. If you've already had other difficult stuff to manage, then you could use some ideas for coping from what you've done before. Then again, you might feel pretty full up with the other tough times and not feel able to do grief on top of that. And, again, go easy on yourself.

Get over it? Deal with it? Move on?

People might also say other things which can be hard to hear. Sometimes it seems as if the rest of the world is telling you to 'get over it' or 'deal with it' or 'move on'. The young people we work with tell us that you don't 'get over' your grief; instead, you learn to live with it and somehow get used to it. They say that no matter what they show on the outside, they are still 'dealing with their grief'. And they add that their grief comes back at times, so it is never really done and 'dealt' with. As for moving on, they tell us that although they want to be able to get on with life, they don't necessarily want to move on if that means leaving the person behind because that person was important.

So if it's not about 'getting over it', what is grief all about?

Young people have told us that for them grieving is a combination of:

- finding ways to cope with the loss
- finding ways to let go of some of the pain
- finding ways to remember and still feel connected to the person who died
- finding ways to still have a good future.

Although there are no fixed 'right' or 'wrong' ways to grieve, there are things that might be making life even harder or even putting you at risk – for example, by doing something that could get you into trouble or things that put you or other people in danger. Sometimes people do risky things because they're feeling so wretched, or because they are just desperate to feel better. That's really understandable.

But risky things are...well, *risky*. There's a risk...there's a chance that something bad will happen. And it might feel as if nothing could be as bad as what has already happened. But as you get through your grief, you'll start to feel less bad and you don't want to have made things worse. If you're feeling so bad that you want to do something risky or harmful, it's worth taking a breath, thinking about your options and letting someone you trust know that you've been feeling like this. Often when people do something risky, they just couldn't see any other way of coping – but if you're reading this book, then you're obviously looking for alternatives, and we think that you can find some (maybe in this book, or maybe elsewhere). If you think this could be happening to you, please tell an adult that you trust. If you're not sure who to tell, try one of the helpline suggestions in Chapter 3 and they will be able to help you work out what to do next.

You don't have to be a scientist to use a theory

In science, they have all sorts of theories that explain stuff – there's a theory of gravity which explains why we don't all float around, there's a theory of evolution which explains how humans developed skills that other animals didn't, there's an atomic theory...but we don't really know what that one explains. Well, there are also theories of grief.

Researchers around the world have studied grief and have some really useful ideas that help to explain what's going on. But they don't say that there is a right or a wrong way of doing grief. One of the weird things about grief is that it affects people in very different ways and at different times. In fact, the word 'grief' is used to describe so many very different reactions that it's almost useless as a word, because it doesn't really mean just one thing.

You may experience some of the same things as your friends and others who are bereaved, but you may also experience some very different things. The theories of grief help us to understand *why* we feel whatever we are feeling when we are grieving, they help us to know what to expect, and they also help us to have some ideas about how to cope with what's going on for us.

There are quite a few different theories about grief, and here we'll explain a few that lots of people find useful. But these are just ideas – they may be ideas based on lots of research, but that does not necessarily mean that they'll work for you. We're not saying that these ideas are definitely *truthful*, just that they might be *useful*.

Dual process theory
Lots of people find this theory useful (that doesn't mean you have to!) and it is based on people's reports of what happened after someone died. It was first suggested by two professors at Utrecht University in the Netherlands.[2] It describes the way that many people adjust to the death of somebody that they care about. This theory suggests that as people adjust to their loss, they alternate between two different ways of coping:

---

2   Stroebe, M. and Schut, H. (1999) 'The dual process model of coping with bereavement: Rationale and description.' *Death Studies 23*, 3, 197–224.

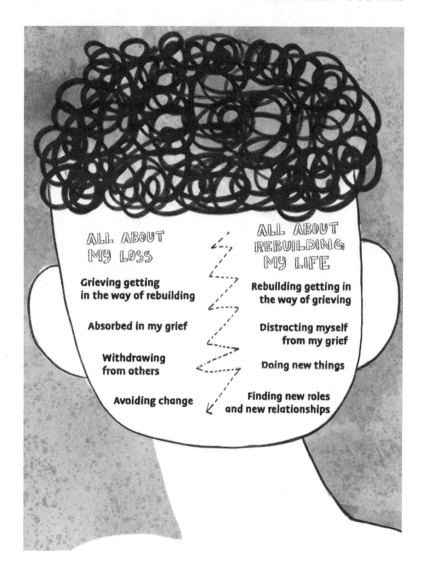

ALL ABOUT MY LOSS

Grieving getting
in the way of rebuilding

Absorbed in my grief

Withdrawing
from others

Avoiding change

ALL ABOUT REBUILDING MY LIFE

Rebuilding getting in
the way of grieving

Distracting myself
from my grief

Doing new things

Finding new roles
and new relationships

FOCUSING ON THE LOSS

One type of coping is all about getting your head around the fact that the person has died. In the theory, they actually call it 'loss-oriented coping', but we're just going to call it focusing on the loss. It generally involves spending time thinking about the person who died, the relationship you had with them, their life, the way that they died, and imagining what they would make of things.

It will probably include being incredibly sad that they have gone and really longing for them, wishing that they were still here. It might involve being angry about the fact that they have died or how they died. It will likely involve reminiscing about moments of the person's life. Sometimes people do the reminiscing together with others, sharing stories about them. Other times, people do the reminiscing on their own, either just remembering certain times or using things such as photos, videos or objects to prompt memories and thoughts.

OLIVIA'S PERSONAL EXPERIENCE

There are a few things I have that remind me of my dad. His guitar, because that's something he taught me to play, and it reminds me of him when I was growing up. I have pictures of us which I keep on my walls, and one of his old jumpers as well as a cowboy hat he wore while working in the garden and garage. These items remind me of him and keep me feeling close to him which is really helpful on days that I really miss him.

I talk to him out loud, too. Sometimes I have a full conversation with him, when I go to see his grave; other times, I just say something out loud when I see things that remind me of him, like the same model of car he drove or when I hear music he liked. Things like this make me feel closer to him again because I can physically see or hold direct reminders of my dad and that can be really helpful when grieving.

FOCUSING ON REBUILDING

But as people adjust to a bereavement, they usually don't just spend all of their time absorbed in focusing on the loss. They usually dip in and dip out of it. And when they are not in the loss-oriented processing, they usually spend some time focusing on rebuilding (in the theory, they call it 'restoration-oriented processing'). This involves making adjustments to their world, so that they can manage now that the person isn't physically in it any more.

It might mean having to develop new routines in the household, or having to learn new skills now that they are no longer there to do things. It could involve having to move house and sorting out belongings. It might involve re-imagining themselves and developing new relationships with other people.

Does any of this sound familiar to you? Do you feel as if you're just swinging from one approach to the other? This seems to be the way that many people move forward and start to get through their grief.

Based on this theory, it makes complete sense that you will have bad days and good days. And that the good days don't mean that you're done with the bad days – it just means that you're alternating. And it also means that when you have a bad day after some good days, you haven't gone backwards – it's actually the way that many people move forwards. Gradually, over time, the pain and overwhelming feelings become less strong, on average.

Tasks of mourning

Have you heard of the different *stages* of grief? The thing is, some people do the stages in a different order and some people miss out stages altogether. The stages are quite specific and do not apply to everyone. So it's not always so useful to think about stages. Professor William Worden worked with lots of bereaved young people in the United States. He didn't describe stages, but he did describe 'tasks of mourning'.[3] It's as if this is the 'work' that bereaved people need to do after someone they love has died.

The 'tasks' are not as specific as stages, and you don't really have to do them in a particular order – in fact, you might find that you do a bit of one, then a bit of another, then go back and do a bit more of the first. It's kind of like having homework to do from four different subjects, and instead of doing all of one subject before moving on to another, you do a bit of one, then a bit of another and then a bit of another, and then back to a bit more of the first one. The four tasks that he described are:

- accept the reality of the loss
- process the pain of grief
- adjust to a world without the person who died

---

3   Worden, J.W. (2018) *Grief Counselling and Grief Therapy. A Handbook for the Mental Health Practitioner* (5th edn). New York, NY: Springer Publishing.

- find a lasting connection with the person who died while continuing with life.

ACCEPT THE REALITY OF THE LOSS

This might sound like a daft one, and if you're bothering to read this book, then you have probably already done this. But not necessarily. For some people, this task can be really difficult. You find the loss just so shocking that you can't quite believe it. And then just when you think that you've accepted that the person has died, the next day you find yourself surprised by it and not quite believing it. It might feel as if you're going mad – but you're not. You're just a normal human being, and normal human beings make automatic assumptions as a way to help us manage life.

We assume that the ground will be firm enough to take our weight, so rather than take each step very carefully to check that the ground is firm enough, we just confidently step forward. It works well as a way to get on with life. When the person was alive, unless they were really ill, you probably didn't go and check to see if they were still alive each morning – you just assumed that they'd be there. That's a pretty sensible way to get on with life – you can't waste hours every morning checking that all the important people are alive – you just make an assumption that they are and get on with things.

So when one of them dies, it makes sense that that's going to be difficult to get your head around. You may have had years of having them around and just got completely used to it. And as well as getting your head around the fact that they are no longer alive, you also have to get your head around the fact that your life will be very different now without them.

So you might need to give yourself a bit of time to complete this task. And if you feel as if you'll never really accept that it's *okay*, over time you will most likely get used to them not being around, even if it remains upsetting.

PROCESS THE PAIN OF GRIEF

Then, as you begin to accept the reality that they have died, you may experience pain. And that pain might be accompanied by all sorts of strong and overwhelming feelings. We've already talked a bit about the different feelings. One of the good things about this particular theory is that it doesn't tell you exactly what feelings you might have. And we like that because the young people we've worked with have had all sorts of different feelings after someone has died.

There are lots of ideas later in this book to help you to cope with different feelings. You might find that you need to do something with these feelings and with the pain, rather than just ignore it and hope that it fades. Remember, this theory describes 'tasks of grief', which sort of implies that there is work to be done here. It's not easy, but it is necessary.

And remember, as we described with the other model, it's not always a smooth ride – it's not as if each day the pain will get steadily easier. It's much more likely that it will come and go, and sometimes just when you think that it's behind you, it suddenly pops up again and seems really difficult. And this might actually be a good thing, because I'm not sure that many of us would manage to do all of this task in one go – personally, I'd much rather dip in and dip out a bit. If you've got a really difficult bit of homework to do, yes, it can be useful to really get stuck in and focus on it for a while. But it might also be useful to have a break and go for a walk before coming back to it.

 Grief

If only

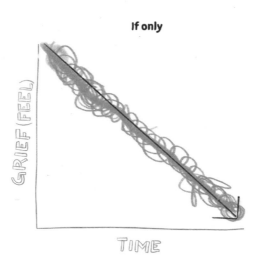

Probably more like this

ADJUST TO A WORLD WITHOUT THE PERSON WHO DIED

There may be some very obvious practical changes that you have to get used to. You may have to change schools, change who you live with, change your normal routines. And all of these will take time to get used to, as you sort of 're-learn' the rules of your new world. These changes are probably not ones that you would have chosen, and it can be infuriating to have to cope with changes caused by an event over which you had no control. Your life might feel completely turned upside down, and it's going to take some getting used to this new way of being.

But as well as obvious practical changes to get used to, there may be other changes that you have to get used to. The person who died might have played a particular role in your life, and now they're not there. Your life is different now; maybe YOU are different now. You may not even have realized how important the person was to you until they died.

But although grief reforms you, it doesn't have to define you. It doesn't have to be the only significant thing in your life that makes up your identity. You can't go back to being as you were before – it's about going forward to how you're going to be.

FIND A LASTING CONNECTION WITH THE PERSON WHO DIED WHILE CONTINUING WITH LIFE

This might seem like a weird one. Or perhaps you are worried that other people will think it's weird. But instead of cutting your relationship with the person who died and just getting used to that, lots of people have found it really helpful to continue to have a relationship with the person who died.

Of course it's a different relationship – it's more inside your head – but they can still play a part in your life.

Lots of young people we work with still talk to the person who died. They may imagine what their person would think about things, and imagine what they would say. Your person can still be a part of your life – just not as big a part as when they were alive.

Some people find it helpful to have a thing that reminds them of their person. It might be a treasured possession like their watch, or a tie, or a photograph, and these objects can be used to bring the person to mind, perhaps remember something nice about them, and keep the relationship current.

Growing around your grief

This is not exactly a theory but more of an idea to explain different ways of understanding grief. It was developed by Lois Tonkin.[4]

You'll see in the following image a set of three jars. Each contains a 'ball' of grief that represents your world and it shows that over time your ball of grief gets smaller, giving you more time to get on with your life. Many people expect that's what will happen when you are grieving, and maybe that is what it's like for some, including you. But lots of young people say their grief doesn't really get smaller.

---

4   Tonkin, L. (1996) 'Growing around grief: Another way of looking at grief and recovery.' *Bereavement Care 15*, 1, 10.

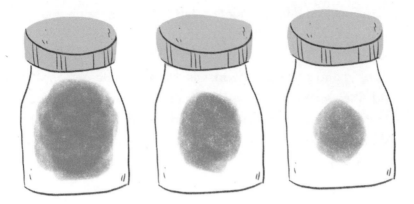

Tonkin's next image of three jars shows that the ball of grief stays the same size, but it is the jars that get bigger over time. This explains how by gradually 'growing your world' and finding new things to fill it with, even though your grief is still present, it doesn't dominate your life in the same way.

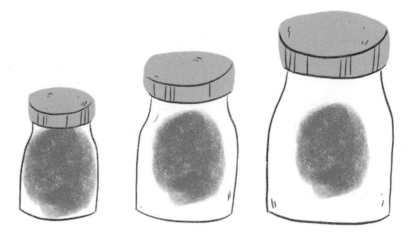

Upward spiral of grief

For a long time, people thought that grief went in stages, where you went through feelings in a particular order and had to do each stage in order. Dr Shelley Gilbert instead suggests that the feelings of grief go round and round like a spiral.[5] And rather than experiencing them in a particular order and then moving on, you instead revisit your feelings. And when those feelings come back around, they might be in varying degrees of heaviness or lightness. Sometimes you will be sad, but a lighter shade of sad than you've been at other times. Other times you might spiral back towards the centre of those heavy feelings because it's a difficult time. This doesn't mean you will always be in the dark centre of grief. You're moving upwards and outwards.

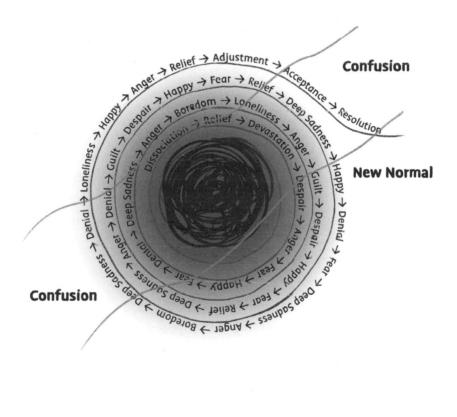

5   Gilbert, S. (2021) *Grief Book*. Grief Encounter Publications.

Finding your own theory or metaphor

We hope there are some things you relate to in this section and that help you make sense of what you're experiencing. You might find that you have your own metaphor that helps.

OLIVIA'S PERSONAL EXPERIENCE

I like to think of my grief like climbing a mountain – lots of different ways to do it will be recommended to you, but in the end, the route you take is your personal choice. And when you start the climb, it might be hard at first, or really easy. But the conditions change, and by the time you've reached the summit, you realize you went up and down, changed course, up and down, got stuck for a bit, up and down again. That's what grief is like. Ever-changing and malleable.

Even after eight years, I still don't really know how I manage my grief. I just sort of do; I talk to people about it, I write my thoughts down, I talk to myself about it and I accept that some days are sad and hard for no reason other than that's my brain telling me it needs to feel those emotions that day.

Like that mountain climb, if you do it again in the future, you might find it easier. The longer you grieve and go through the process, the less intense those feelings will be and you will begin to see and feel the healing.

Complications

Feelings about the person who died not 100% positive

What happens if you didn't have a good relationship with the person who died? Sometimes that makes it even more difficult.

Even when we love and care about people, most relationships aren't 100% positive all the time. As part of everyday life, we will often disagree with others. Families who spend a lot of time together are likely to irritate each other at least sometimes and often a lot of the time. In spite of this, after a death we can usually still hold on to a sense of loving them and being loved by them. And so, in our grief, we can at least hold on to the loving part.

However, sometimes relationships can be a lot more difficult, and this can make grieving the loss of that person tricky. It can feel pretty confusing to feel so much grief when you are not sure about the strength of the relationship you had with them. Maybe there were a lot of differences and arguments between you both – it can be hard knowing that these can no longer be resolved.

66 I'd always had a pretty good relationship with my dad from when I was young. Even after my parents separated, I spent lots of time at his flat and got on with my new step-mum. However, Dad found it very difficult to handle things when I told him I was in a same-sex relationship with a girl. We had some heated conversations and I stopped visiting him because I felt so hurt by his reaction to me. And then Dad died suddenly from a heart

attack. I was left not only grieving for Dad but desperately sad about how strained our relationship had been and it was more complicated because of how rejected I felt. For some time, I couldn't find a way to even get comfort from my early memories. (Scarlett)

OLIVIA'S PERSONAL EXPERIENCE

My grief surrounding my dad's death has been hard to navigate at times, because I didn't always have a happy relationship with him. He could be very mean to my mum, me and my siblings, and he worked a lot and spent lots of time in his garage working on cars and bikes, or playing the guitar in another room. So even when he was around, it sometimes seemed like he wasn't.

He wasn't often very open about his feelings and emotions, so even when he wasn't being mean, it was hard to know how he was feeling. This made it very hard after he died, because I felt so much sadness and love, but I was also reminded in my own mind and by other people of all the horrible things I had seen and heard. It made it very confusing for me, and I remember at times feeling guilty for being sad because some people weren't as sad, and I felt guilty for not being sad enough at other times because I told myself I should be. I would catch myself laughing and talking to friends, and immediately feel guilty as though someone would tell me I was wrong for not grieving the 'right way'.

But your relationship with the person you lose is

personal. Someone else's experience with that person is not the same as yours, and you don't owe anyone an explanation for your grief and how you go through it. The not so nice memories exist alongside the nicer ones, but they don't cancel each other out, and I can accept that both exist because that's who my dad was. I can still feel sad that he isn't here and for the loss of the nicer memories, and I can also be angry and sad about the not so nice ones because they were experiences that shaped my relationship with him.

Over time I have had days, months where I am just angry at him, and others where I only feel love and grieve the physical loss. These changes are as fluid as the changes in my emotions towards him when he was alive, and that tells me that my grief is doing exactly what it is supposed to do.

Sometimes we can feel guilty about things we did or didn't say, or did or didn't do. Maybe the person treated you badly, or treated people you care about badly, and this can make you feel quite muddled about what to do with your feelings. Maybe the person had been absent from your life for a long time – or even throughout your life – and yet you still feel something quite deep on hearing about their death. Ted Bowman, a grief educator, describes this as shattered dreams[6] – grieving for the hopes and dreams for a future you now cannot have with that person. Liam experienced this when grieving for his mum:

---

6   Bowman, T. (2018) *Finding Hope When Dreams Have Shattered.* CreateSpace Independent Publishing Platform.

" When my mum died it was complicated. I was cross that she could have stopped the drinking that killed her but didn't. I was also devastated that there was no chance of her ever getting better and us having a good relationship together. And now I'll never know what it is like to have a mum who can look after me properly. (Liam)

" My grandad was really harsh with me and my brother, and we used to dread going to visit him. When he died, I couldn't understand why I felt so upset as he'd always been mean to me, but somehow, I still missed him. (Emily)

OLIVIA'S PERSONAL EXPERIENCE

I had a tricky relationship with my dad, which was more negative than positive. I felt as though I was lying to myself about missing him and almost trying to convince myself that people wouldn't believe me when I did talk to friends about it, because the little bits they did know about him and our relationship were not nice. It was very hard. It still can be. One moment I can talk about a happy memory and the next be sad about something that reminds me of the unpleasant bits, and it feels very confusing to not know why I feel those feelings when I do. But you can't question your grief. You just have to allow yourself to feel all of the emotions and understand that you don't have to know why, you just do.

When a relationship hasn't been 100% positive, it doesn't necessarily mean it was 100% negative. Maybe there were some okay bits and even some good or special bits.

Psychologist Julie Stokes,[7] who set up a bereavement service called Winston's Wish, uses stones to help young people work out their different feelings and memories:

- **Rocky stone** represents all the rough, sharp parts of the relationship and maybe some really difficult memories.
- **Smooth stone** represents some everyday memories that weren't very special, but also weren't too rough.
- **Shiny stone** represents the special moments and memories.

Maybe your relationship with the person who died is a combination of all these stones. It is okay to acknowledge the tough parts, but it is also completely fine to have the okay bits and even hold on to a special memory or two. We hope you have people around you who can support you to do this.

Traumatic deaths

What happens if the way that the person died was traumatic for you? Sometimes that makes it more difficult to be sad about the loss, because you're too busy thinking about the death itself. Perhaps you saw or heard something that was really upsetting when the person died. Maybe you have imagined it in your mind from the information you've been given. If you don't have all the information about what happened to the person, you might be trying really hard to make sense of it, but it's difficult to do this without enough information. Adults often want to protect you from knowing

7   Stokes, J. and Stubbs, D. (2008) *Beyond the Rough Rock* (2nd edn). Gloucester: Winston's Wish.

some difficult stuff – sometimes this can mean that you naturally create lots of possible scenarios and they may not be true. Even if you don't need or want to have every detail, at least being able to know the when, where and how can be a start. Having this information probably won't be *easier* or *better* but might be *less bad* than imagining lots of different things. And *knowing* means that you can work towards making sense of the death and coping with your grief.

If the adults you live with are finding it difficult to communicate with you about the death, then you could try telling them why it's so important for you to know. Maybe another trusted adult could help you with this conversation – a youth worker or someone from your school perhaps. Some bereavement charities we've listed in Chapter 3 can help adults with how to find words to talk about a death. You could also show the adults in your home this page in the book – or leave it open with a large red arrow pointing to this paragraph (not subtle, but possibly effective!). Alternatively, here are a few ways you might start a conversation:

- Can we find a time to talk about what happened to Dad?
- I'm still a bit confused about when Sofia died. Can you help?
- I've got some questions about Mum going round and round in my head. Can I ask you?

Very occasionally, no one really knows what did happen or sometimes you have to wait for quite a while until the coroner puts together all the evidence and gives their verdict.

The waiting and the uncertainty are likely to add more distress to an already painful situation.

It is normal to become really upset when a death was traumatic for you – all sorts of things can act as triggers that leave you feeling as if it is happening all over again. The thing about traumatic memories is that they are not like memories for other events. If someone asked you about the last time you went to the cinema, you would find your cinema memory, bring it into mind and tell the story. You might not remember the 'data' of the event (sights, smells, sounds, tastes, touches, thoughts, feelings), but you can remember the story of it. Memories for traumatic events are different.

Instead of being made up of words and stories that are complete and make sense, traumatic memories are made up of the data. And instead of being recalled when you choose to bring it to mind, traumatic memories are very easily triggered – they might even seem as if they have a bit of a life of their own. And instead of being coherent and complete, traumatic memories can be made up of individual fragments.

When the traumatic memories intrude, it can feel as if you are re-experiencing the events rather than remembering the memory. Because these memories are so horrible and seem out of control, people invest a lot of time and energy in trying *not* to think about them. But that rarely works. In fact, it usually makes it worse. It's like a boomerang – the harder you throw it away, the harder it comes back and hits you.

Sometimes getting on with grief involves bringing the

person who died to mind and remembering something about their life. But if the way that they died was traumatic, then whenever you try to remember them, you can find that the memories of the way that they died push out the other memories of their life.

Over time, these traumatic memories of the death often start to decrease, and you find you have room in your mind to think about the person and be sad without being so scared. Sometimes, though, the traumatic memories get stuck, and people can need some extra help with their grief. If this sounds like you, then talk to an adult you trust or get some help from one of the organizations in Chapter 3.

Sometimes it's hard for the people around you at home and at school to talk to you about what happened, and so you find you're carrying it around on your own. Others can think (mistakenly) that not talking about it will be easier. But never talking about it can give the traumatic memories too much power and can make it easier for them to keep coming back into your mind. Instead, finding a way to let the memories in and putting them into words that you speak or write can make it less bad and give you back some control (there is lots of research that shows this). It will never be fine that the person died, but it should become less difficult to cope with, giving you more room in your life for some good stuff.

With a traumatic death, there can often be a lot of extra things to have to manage, especially when lots of people know about it. This could include the police or the courts, and sometimes families have to cope with the death being in the media. Just when a family wants some privacy to make sense of what has happened, it can be in the news and on social media. It might also be reported in a way that doesn't feel true or kind.

Death by suicide

This particular type of bereavement is very often considered to be traumatic. Being bereaved by suicide can be a particularly difficult thing to get through and often brings with it very intense emotions. You might be feeling confused because you can't understand why they would have done that. You could feel guilty because you think it was your fault in some way, or anxious about whether or not you or someone else in your family will do the same thing. You might be feeling incredibly alone. You might be feeling angry because of what they did, and then guilty because you were feeling angry.

Sometimes being bereaved by suicide can be particularly tough because other people may not want to talk about it, and you may feel as if you are left on your own to deal with your grief. Sometimes adults find it too difficult to talk about, and so they sometimes avoid letting people know that the person died by suicide – if they didn't actually tell you, you might have found out some other way. And if you don't want to talk about it, you could find yourself becoming isolated from your friends and family.

You may feel as if nobody has ever been through anything like what you're going through, and you may be wondering if you can actually cope with it. No two bereavements are the same, but we have worked with a lot of young people who have been bereaved by suicide, and although it's been a particularly rocky road for lots of them, they have coped. The sections about what to do in Chapter 2 are just as applicable to those of you bereaved by suicide as they are for other bereavements.

OLIVIA'S PERSONAL EXPERIENCE

My father took his own life, and a traumatic death cause can add to the shock you already feel about the loss. I was only 13 when it happened, and I didn't know how he had died right away. Looking back, that was a helpful way for me to process the death because I would have been very overwhelmed questioning the cause, on top of all of the questions I had already about him not coming home and not seeing him again.

As I got older and naturally knew/had learned more than I did when I was young about life in general, I started asking questions from which I learned a lot, and this affected my grief by raising more questions in my head and giving me more answers to process.

It was hard. Some questions I asked my mum, I thought I was ready for the answers to, but I really wasn't and that affected how I healed and grieved. I still have so many questions all these years later, and unfortunately, I won't ever hear the answers to some of them, which is hard. It can feel at times like there was no closure to the loss and no real end, because I didn't see it coming. But even if I had known he was going to pass, I would still have had questions to ask.

Suicide was a hard cause of death to hear, and it was easy for me to get overwhelmed by what I, or other people, could have done. But in your grief you have to focus on the memories you have of the person and how you are going to heal. You cannot change anything else, and you will only disrupt your own journey by contemplating things out of your control.

My father's death by suicide was not something my younger siblings knew about either. They just knew that he had died, and my mum wouldn't have been able to explain to children what had happened in a way that would make sense to them. But being slightly older, when I did ask and was told, it felt as though I was grieving all over again but in a slightly different way. I felt knocked back with this added layer of reality about the loss, and I felt like I could now explain and understand parts of my grief and emotions and memories with this cause being told to me.

I was worried after I found out though because I didn't know who had this information. I was worried about how people would look at me and my family because of it. I had a friend whose father had passed away from an illness, and she was very open about it because she said it was common, and they had known it was going to happen. But all I felt was shame and embarrassment that people would look at me differently if I told them how my father had died.

I was angry – my dad didn't have to die. I didn't have to feel this sad and miss him. He made a choice and I had to deal with the aftermath. These feelings are completely normal and fair. But it still hurt to think that it didn't have to happen. This aspect of my grief was a hard one to pass through, but I did it because I needed to heal and grow, because my life is present and ongoing.

Disenfranchised grief

What happens if those around you aren't very supportive of your grief – maybe they think you should be over it by now, maybe they don't understand (or know) that the person was important to you. Sometimes other people have a bad opinion of the person who died and that can make it hard for you to grieve openly and get support. They might say negative or judgemental things about the person who died and not realize how hard it is for you to hear them. When you feel as though you're the only one who is grieving, it can be pretty lonely.

❝ My dad left when I was little and although he planned to visit me, I only ever got to see him every year or so and then he'd disappear, and I wouldn't hear from him for ages. When I heard he'd died, I felt really muddled up. Why did I miss him so much when I didn't really know him? (Chao-Xing)

Sometimes adults can think that children and young people are too young to really understand what has happened. They can minimize or dismiss the feelings of grief, believing that being younger somehow protects you from understanding and therefore protects you from the pain. People grieve at all ages – from the very youngest to the very oldest.

Disenfranchised grief can also occur when no one else knows that the person who died was important to you. This can happen when there is a death in your school or college. Relationships are entirely individual, and even people we didn't know personally very well can still be important to us and their death can trigger a wave of unexpected grief.

Maybe the person who died was friendly to you when you first joined the school. Perhaps you used to sit next to each other in science and shared the same jokes about the lessons. You may have developed feelings for the person who died and had hoped or dreamed of getting close to them. Often the focus of attention at school is on the people who everyone thinks are closest to the person who died – this could mean you are not involved in ways to remember them and might not be offered support automatically.

66 When Muna died, everyone was really shocked, and the school set up a memory book (which I didn't know what to write in) and organized a memorial service (which I was too upset to go to). Her friends were offered the chance to see the school counsellor and all the teachers kept an eye on them. No one knew how I felt about Muna – we'd only exchanged a few texts, but I really liked her. I didn't feel that I could tell my family how bad I felt because it wasn't like she was actually my girlfriend. (Ben)

The death of a school teacher or an adult who helped you can be really tough, especially when people don't recognize what was so important about the relationship and why it's so tough for you.

66 Mr Layne was my geography teacher, and even though I only saw him a couple of times a week, he had always been really

supportive of me and would ask about my brother who had the same disability as his brother. He would also rib me if his team beat mine in the football. When I heard that he died in an accident, I was completely gutted. I also couldn't get his brother out of my head – wondering how he was now, too. After a few days, school seemed to go back to normal and I felt like I was just expected to get on and get used to having a new geography teacher. I couldn't face geography any more, so I just missed lessons by having the day off, going to medical or staying with my student support manager. (Malik)

Your grief is still important and your feelings are still valid even if no one else recognizes this. Disenfranchised grief often happens because people do not know or do not appreciate how big the death is for you.

66 When I eventually spoke to my Head of Year about it, they wanted to understand why I kept missing lessons. When I said it was hard to have a different geography teacher, she did get it and she wanted to know how school could help me. She also told me she had been to Mr Layne's funeral and got to meet his brother. Just knowing that she was trying to understand me somehow made me feel a bit better. (Malik)

Perhaps try to explain to someone you trust that this person was important to you and their death has been affecting you deeply. This could be a friend, someone you live with or someone from school or college. There are also places where you can be supported with making sense of your grief (see Chapter 3).

Chapter 2

HOW TO MAKE IT LESS BAD

The young people we've worked with have often found that they've needed some help with particular features of their grief. And we've got a separate section on several of these. But there are two things that seem to help with many of these features – *meaning making* and *social support*. So let's think about them first.

Meaning making

Have you ever noticed how two different people can see exactly the same thing but make something completely different of it? You and a friend both see the same tackle in a football match, and you think it was just a firm fair challenge, whereas your friend sees it as an outrageous foul and can't believe that you see it differently. Or you and a friend watch an episode of a reality TV show in which one person ends a relationship with someone else. You think that it was done quite nicely and shows what a nice person they are, with integrity and honesty, whereas your friend shrieks obscenities at the TV, calling the person a variety of rude names. Same event, same context; but very different meaning making. All sorts of things can influence how you and your friends see things.

This same meaning making applies to how you make sense of the death and your grief. And how you make sense of things will massively affect how you feel, and what you do. Over time, the way that you make sense of things will change.

Perhaps you think that the death means that your life is ruined, or that you just can't cope without the person, or that everyone in your life is going to leave. Those would be pretty catastrophic meanings and would be likely to cause a lot of upset. And then there is the question of how you make sense of your upset. Do you think that it means that you can't cope or that you'll never feel happy again? If that is how you make sense of things, then you're likely to get even more upset.

66 Lucie kept thinking about the big argument she had with Mum the day before she died. Lucie had said some mean things, and so had her mum, actually. Now she couldn't get her thoughts about how stressed her mum had been. 'That row was just the kind of stress that the doctor had said Mum needed to avoid. But then I started on her. I can never forgive myself for causing Mum's death and ruining life for the whole family.'

One of the 'traps' that people fall into sometimes is that they get so upset because of the meaning that they've made of something that they push the hard thoughts away and don't really give themselves a chance to think things through and re-evaluate them. If you think that your life is ruined because the person died, then that is such a distressing thought that you just want to push it away rather than think it through. Whereas if you are able to tolerate some of the distress and start to think things through, even just a little bit, you may find that you create a new meaning. For example, you start to think that, yes, your life will be very different without the person who died, and some of your plans will be different, and that is really sad. But then you start to realize that you can make other plans, or that some things will still be the same.

Some of the young people we work with even end up taking some positive things from the death – that's not to say that they think it's a good thing that it happened. But they end up being more appreciative of the people they still have in their lives. Or they realize how everyone is going to die and so they should make the most of their life.

Sometimes people around you will try to help you to see things differently – but you might not be ready to hear other people's ideas, and they may not fit for you anyway. But one way that you can help your own meaning making develop and adapt is to start to notice it and reflect on it. It may seem a bit weird, but what we're suggesting here is that you try to think about your thinking. Become a sort of detective to try to piece together the clues that will explain what's going on inside your head and your body.

1. Hold that thought

It can really help sometimes to write this down and try to pinpoint the thoughts or beliefs behind your overwhelming feelings.

It can also help to see your thoughts and beliefs as just that – thoughts and beliefs. They may not *necessarily* be true (maybe that person in the TV show *was* a complete waster for dumping the other person). Thoughts are not facts.

" Lucie's thought: 'Mum died because I argued with her.'

2. Gently think about and around those thoughts

Have a look at your thoughts and beliefs if you've written them down. What happens when you see them there in words?

And then just very gently think those thoughts and beliefs through. Try asking the following questions:

- Do you think them *all* the time, or do they come and go?
- How much do you believe that your thoughts or beliefs are true, and does that amount go up and down?
- Are you being a bit hard on yourself?
- Are you being a bit hard on someone else?
- Are you thinking in all-or-nothing terms, when in fact it is a bit more complicated than that?
- Are you accurate in your evaluations, or are you minimizing or over-stating things?
- Are you over-generalizing?
- Are you considering all sides of things, or just focusing on one side?

- Are you putting yourself under an unfair amount of pressure?
- If a friend said they were thinking that, what would you say to them?

66 Lucie thought it through: 'I think about this a lot of the time, especially when something else has gone wrong. I always believe that it's true. I guess I'm being a bit hard on myself. But it's difficult to go easy on yourself when your mum has died. I'd probably tell my friend that even though you argued with your mum, it was the heart condition that killed her, not you.'

3. Any alternatives?

Are there other ways of seeing things? You don't have to believe them, they may not fit for you, but just stop and think if there are any other ways of seeing things. What would happen if you were to take on some of those alternatives, even if only some of the time? Would that make things better or worse for you?

We're not suggesting that this will help you to magically see things differently and that suddenly all will be well. But we are suggesting that this can help you to see things in a more nuanced way that is probably more realistic, and ultimately more helpful.

66 Lucie's alternatives: 'Although I know the row wasn't good, it wasn't what killed her. Mum did have a heart condition and that wasn't anything to do with me – she had that since she was a child. My aunt says how special my relationship with my mum was. Maybe I could try to focus on that a bit more.'

Social support

The other thing that seems to help with lots of the troubles of grief is social support. Different people get their social support from different people – there is no one best formula that works for everyone. Some people have lots of friends; others have just one or two. Some are very well supported by their family, others not so much. It seems that having other people around you and offering various different types of support can be extremely helpful in getting on with your grief. The trick is to stop and think about what support you get from who, and how can you make the most of that support.

Who's on your side?

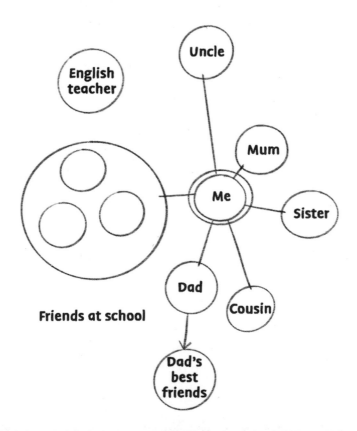

First of all, who have you got on your side? Who are all of the people (and animals) who support you? Perhaps try to map this out in some way. You could create an 'ecomap' – this looks like a mind map, but instead of ideas, you map out the people who are around you. Or write your initials in the middle of a piece of paper, draw a couple of circles around it and then write the initials of the different people who are important in your life. Or imagine yourself picking your ultimate team for your favourite sport. Who would you choose who shows up and you can rely on? They will each play a different role in your life, but together they make a great team for you.

See if there is anyone you've left out and add them. But when it comes to social support, quality is more important than quantity, especially when it comes to helping you get through.

OLIVIA'S PERSONAL EXPERIENCE

This can be really helpful for when your grief gets overwhelming and heavy. Having a map of the people you can turn to in front of you is a much easier way to see who can support you when you need it most, rather than trying to think when your head is already confused and occupied.

Who plays what role?

Once you've got everyone listed, make a note of who plays what role. Does one friend cheer you up and make you laugh, does another help with your homework, does another help you think through your problems? Does one parent help you with practical stuff, and the other help with emotional stuff?

Do you need to shift the team around a bit or give them some coaching?

When you look at your map, does it seem about right for you at the moment, or would you like to make some changes? Are there some people you ought to be having a bit less to do with at the moment, and some you could do with pulling in a bit closer? And do some of them need some clear guidelines about what you need from them? We're not talking about being demanding and bossy; we're just talking about making sure that those people who care about you and might want to help have some ideas of how they can help. For example:

66 Dad – 'I don't need you trying to fix it or cheer me up.'

66 Sam – 'I don't want to talk about it right now. Can we just go out and have some fun?'

66 Abi – 'I could really do with telling you what's going on. You don't have to fix it; you just have to listen and not be put off by me crying.'

OLIVIA'S PERSONAL EXPERIENCE

It can be very empowering in your grief to tell people when they are and are not helping. If someone is giving you solutions when you just wanted to talk about your feelings, it's okay to remind them that you don't want them to fix it – you just want them to listen. Those you trust and love are also figuring it out as they go, like you are with your grief. They might think you want solutions when you just want to let it out, and it's okay to remind them and tell them that, so they can help you as you grieve and heal. Only you know how you are feeling inside – if something isn't helping, then you can vocalize that.

Ideas for coping with sadness and feeling low

Feeling sad and low is a natural part of grieving the loss of someone significant. Even though feeling sad can be really uncomfortable and heavy, it's probably not realistic to be able to avoid sadness altogether. So in this chapter we'll think about learning to carry heavy feelings of sadness and finding ways to express them, and also about developing strategies to help you have some time off from your grief if things are getting more difficult to cope.

Waves of sadness

Some people have described grieving as being on the seashore with the tide of grief coming in and out. There's nothing you can do to stop the grief, just as you can't control the waves.

At times your grief feels further away, although you can see it in the distance and know it's there. Sometimes your grief comes and it's gentle and just tickles your toes. Sometimes the grief is a bit higher like waves that make you have to hold steady to keep your balance from being knocked over.

At other times, though, your grief can feel really rough and strong with crashing waves that knock you off your feet and immerse you in the sea. Maybe you get back on your feet yourself, and maybe there is someone to help you.

If this makes sense to you, use the illustration below and write on times when you have experienced each wave of grief. What size wave was it when you first heard that they had died? At the funeral? When you see something that reminds you of them? When someone asked you about them? What's it been like for you over the last few days?

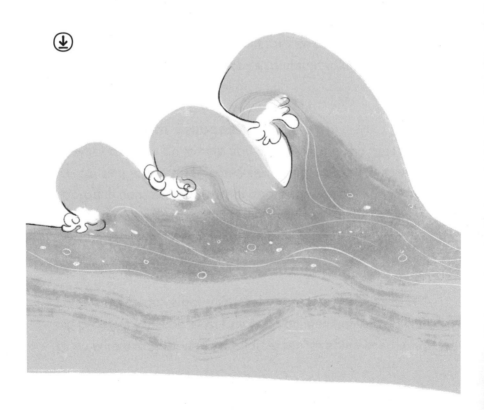

Although we've called this section 'ideas for coping with sadness and feeling low', sad is a bit of a rubbish word as it's used for so many everyday things that happen:

- I'm sad that my football match has been cancelled.
- I'm sad because I've just dropped my pizza, and now the dog has eaten it.
- I'm sad because my best friend seems to be spending more time with other people.

And then people go and use the same word to try to describe the enormous, debilitating and intense feelings of loss when someone has died. We're not sure that the word 'sad' is really *big* enough or *strong* enough to really get to the heart of grief.

Maybe some of these words have more meaning for you:

despairing

heavy-hearted melancholic

gloomy despondent inconsolable

sorrowful distressed out of sorts upset

devastated down

unhappy

Earlier, we thought a lot about why bereavement is so hard, so it makes sense that any or all of these words can describe how you have been feeling at times. And that's the really important phrase here – 'at times'. Although it is really tough to feel like this, it is natural.

Remember that you may be grieving for the memories you had, for the loss you are feeling right now and for the future that may look so very different without the person who has died. That can feel pretty heavy, but we hope that these aren't the only feelings you have. And we hope that at times you can experience some different feelings including moments of joy, fun, energy and relaxation, so that you can have some 'time off' from the intense sadness and that it doesn't overwhelm you often.

Young people we have worked with have found a number of ways to help them cope when they are feeling low or sad. Sadly, none of these ideas actually gets rid of heavy feelings altogether, but there are ways to help you carry these heavy feelings of grief. Have a read through and see which you would like to try.

Rating your sadness

A first step is to get a better handle on your sadness so that you understand it and can recognize how and when it is impacting your day. You can do this by creating your own system for rating these heavy feelings. Maybe like a thermometer. Then you choose the words that best describe your range of feelings – from feeling good, then the lightest drop of feeling a bit down, through to the deepest distress of your heavy heart.

You can keep it simple like this:

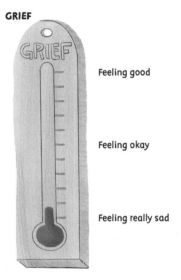

Or if words aren't your thing, maybe you prefer numbers. How good is your mood?

Or use some powerful and personal words like this:

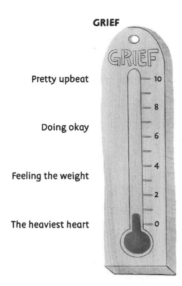

You can also add colour or shades of a colour to show the depth of your feelings.

Once you've created your own system for rating these feelings, you can start working out how deep and heavy the sadness is so that you are beginning to understand grief. One of the trickiest things about feeling low is that when you are really sad or distressed, it can be really hard to remember that you ever felt differently. You can begin to think that you have always felt like this and worry that you will always feel this way.

To help with this, try making a record of your feelings, marking the date next to the appropriate rating on your thermometer. Even better would be to record your highest and lowest score for each day, because usually we don't stay with exactly the same feeling all day. We have higher points (even if only ever so slightly) and maybe sometimes some lower points. Then you can really see how you are doing rather than relying on the memory of your feelings, which isn't always the most accurate.

Making sense of what makes you sad

Can you work out when you feel most sad? Try using your rating or recording method to help you understand and notice when your feelings are at their heaviest. Were there things that happened that day that made it a really low day? Maybe something triggered you? Maybe the date was the anniversary of something? Or the date something would have happened if the person was still alive? Maybe someone said something mean? Or maybe your sadness just came and was hard to shift?

Making sense of what keeps you sad

Think about what you were doing and whether that helped you or made it harder. Sometimes when you are grieving and it's feeling hard and heavy, you might withdraw from others and spend more time alone. Maybe you don't feel interested or excited about seeing your friends, or going to your boxing club or spending time with family. Maybe you think they won't want to spend time with you because you look so miserable.

The trouble with being alone a lot is that it can keep the sadness all around you and not give you a chance to feel anything different. Sometimes that is just what you need for a while, to feel the sadness and grieve your loss because it is important to you.

Sitting with your sadness

Finding a way to sit with these feelings of sadness is a part of getting on with grief. So rather than being scared by heavy feelings or wanting to push them away, when those feelings of pain come, you can find ways to express them, learn to tolerate them and understand them for what they are. As Olivia says, 'Take your sad days and allow them to happen.'

USING MUSIC

Some young people tell us that music is a great way to connect with their grief, whether it is listening to music or playing it themselves. To help you sit with your sadness, make a playlist of songs that match your mood. These are songs you can relate to as they seem to express what you've been thinking or feeling. If you play an instrument (however well or badly), play the song yourself. Or maybe compose your own music or write your own song.

It is also a good idea to work out when you have had enough of carrying this sadness.

Maybe the intensity naturally passes, or you notice it getting less bad as the wave of grief starts to subside. Perhaps you can do something to help it on its way. Try setting yourself a timer on your phone that goes off after three songs, or 30 minutes, or whatever is enough for you. We'll think a bit later on about things to do to help give you time off your sadness. Maybe include a second playlist that helps change your mood – music that is pretty much guaranteed to energize you, make you smile, uplift you or feed your soul.

USING WORDS

We've already mentioned using words to rate and describe your feelings, but you can, of course, go much further and really unpack what these feelings are like and how they are affecting you. Write about what has triggered this wave of sadness and give your grief the attention it deserves. If your tears come when you are feeling sad, then you could even write down what your tears would say if they could talk.

If my tears could talk, they would say:

These words can be an outpouring of sadness all over the page without having to worry about spelling or handwriting or structure (apologies to your English teacher), but they could also be a journal or diary that you complete daily or whenever works for you. Or a story about you and your loss. Or a fictional story about a character going through something like you are. Or a poem.

OLIVIA'S PERSONAL EXPERIENCE

I found it hard after my dad died to let my emotions out with my hobbies and interests, because we shared a lot of interests, like music. But I have always journalled and enjoyed writing, so for me that was something that I kept doing, even when I didn't feel like it, because I knew it would help me to get it out, and I didn't always feel like talking to someone to feel better.

USING MOVEMENT
You can walk or run out your sadness, setting yourself a time or distance to cover while you give your sadness some attention. Try dancing, boxing or any sport to help with your distress. Being outside in the fresh air, whatever the weather, can be especially helpful for your mood.

USING ART
Use art to express how you are feeling, painting messy splodges of colour to represent your mood, or random designs of shapes to focus you, or a detailed illustration of your emotions or memories. Sometimes your mood will be really low when you begin, but young people tell us that by the time they have worked on their art, their mood has shifted and some light has started to come in.

Stuck in the sadness

We mentioned before that these heavy feelings of grief are natural, but there will be times when you want to have some 'time off' your sadness. This doesn't mean that you have forgotten what happened or are not respecting the person who died, but it's important to look after yourself and have a rest from the heaviness you've been carrying. This is a bit like the dual process model that we wrote about in Chapter 1. It describes doing some of your grief but then shifting your focus to rebuilding your life.

People around you will notice if you are showing how low you are feeling. They may try to help because they care. Sometimes they tell you to stop dwelling on what has happened, or to try to think about the happy times. It can be hard to simply *think* differently when you're feeling low. Some may suggest that you try to change your feelings and focus on happiness instead of grief. In practice, it is really difficult to *feel* differently. The way we think, feel and act are all related, and you might get stuck in a bit of a cycle which just keeps going.

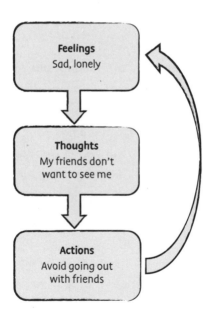

Feelings
Sad, lonely

Thoughts
My friends don't
want to see me

Actions
Avoid going out
with friends

Rebuilding your life

Research has shown that for many young people who are struggling with feeling low, doing something different is an easier first step. And doing something different can gradually help you to think differently and feel differently. Doing something different can be an important step in rebuilding your life. It's not really a case of one trip to the cinema and, wow, the grief has disappeared. Instead, it's gradually putting in activities that give you the chance to feel more positive feelings, to start to balance out the heaviness.

When we say add *activities*, these don't need to be spectacular and magnificent efforts to do ultra-marathons, climb mountains or build an orphanage in a remote village. Although if someone is offering you a weekend break to a tropical island, by all means give it a go! One way of thinking about activities to help rebuild your life is to consider things that give you a sense of

- achievement
- connection or
- enjoyment.

For example, revising for your algebra test might give you a sense of achievement but not necessarily enjoyment, unless numbers are your thing!

Playing online with friends can give you a sense of connection (and we don't mean a good Wi-Fi connection), but spending time actually hanging out with your mates and going to the movies can give you a much higher sense of connection.

You'll no doubt have a number of things in your life that give you a sense of enjoyment even if you haven't been doing them much recently. Maybe watching your dog doing his crazy turn as he tries to catch his tail.

And, of course, some things will tick more than one box – for example, when Lucie rejoined her football team, she found that she got a sense of *achievement* from taking part and assisting in the final goal of the match, a sense of *connection* in seeing her team mates again and a sense of *enjoyment* that had been missing since her mum died. Although she hadn't expected to feel a bit better, she really did. It didn't stop her grieving and missing her mum, but it did start to help.

Of course, rebuilding your life needs more than a couple of bricks. So Lucie found that she had to build on this and keep going to training and matches to carry on balancing with the pain of her loss.

It can really help to make a note of what you did and record how much of a sense of achievement, connection and enjoyment it gives you. This could be on a simple chart like the one here. Score each activity out of 10 or come up with a system that works for you. Or just make a note of it on your phone.

Activity	Achievement	Connection	Enjoyment
Football match	9	8	9
Tidying my room	7	0	-5
Shopping with my aunt	5	8	7

The thing with feeling low is that it can become all-consuming and make you feel as though you've only ever felt this way. Keeping a note of how you got on planning and doing your chosen activities can help build up some evidence of how you *felt* when you *did* these things. And then, next time when your mood is trying to convince you that it's just not worth it, you can remind yourself that it was okay. Or maybe slightly better than okay.

Reduced opportunities

When someone has died, life often changes a lot and you can find that certain activities you used to enjoy are no longer available to you. This might only be temporary or it may be a change that has to stick. The cost might be too much if your family is under more financial pressure. There may be practical barriers to stop you, like getting a lift. Or maybe your enjoyment of an activity was pretty dependent on doing it with the person who died. You need to be creative to work out what activities are available to you even if some of those you previously enjoyed aren't.

One of the things about sadness when you are grieving is that sometimes it's not straightforward. In fact, you can feel sad and happy at the same time – and then a bit confused because those are supposed to be opposite emotions! For example, when Lucie went shopping with her aunt, she did feel sad because she missed her mum as this was something they had enjoyed together. At the same time, though, she did feel a bit happy to get to spend time with her aunt, her mum's younger sister. Somehow it made her feel closer to her mum, too – and it was pretty good to be spoilt with a few treats!

Have you experienced opposite emotions at the same time? Maybe, like Lucie, happiness and sadness? Or maybe more like cross and funny? It can be strange, but grief is a bit strange and not everything about it makes sense.

No one thing works for everyone – try a few to find out what works for you. Even if all these suggestions seem rubbish, maybe it will prompt some of your own ideas that suit you better.

Ideas for coping with anger

Lots of people have found that feeling angry is a big part of grieving. It is also a really natural feeling to have, for all sorts of reasons. This section isn't about telling you not to be angry (you may well have people around who are telling you that). We hope that in giving your angry feelings a bit of time and attention here, you will understand this feeling a bit more. And then you can begin to manage feeling cross in ways that don't end up with anyone getting hurt or you getting into trouble.

Why do we get angry?

Our brains are wired to detect threat and keep us safe. There's a part of the brain called the amygdala (there's actually two of them, but everyone seems to talk just about one) which plays a crucial role in noticing potential threats and triggering the fight–flight–freeze response. This overrides everything else at that moment. We might typically:

- fight – start arguing or getting physical, sometimes with the person or our bedroom door
- flight – run away from the threat, which could be heading to our room or walking out of class
- freeze – become immobile and rooted to the spot.

When we need to protect ourselves from a potential threat, these responses are really helpful and could save our life – or those of others around us. But the amygdala operates on a 'just in case' basis – so 'just in case' the situation is dangerous, the amygdala activates the response designed to keep you safe, without stopping to check out if the threat is real. That means that our brains tend to act now and think later. Sometimes this means that our response is out of proportion to the situation, and we can wonder if we overreacted. Other times, the situation that triggered our anger was truly difficult and in fact our anger was completely fair enough. The trick is not to suppress anger, but to keep it in check so that we can use it.

So what has anger got to do with grief?

First, anger is the bit that people often see, but often there are other feelings that have been bubbling away underneath that made getting frustrated that bit easier or quicker. Maybe there are some feelings here that you have been experiencing:

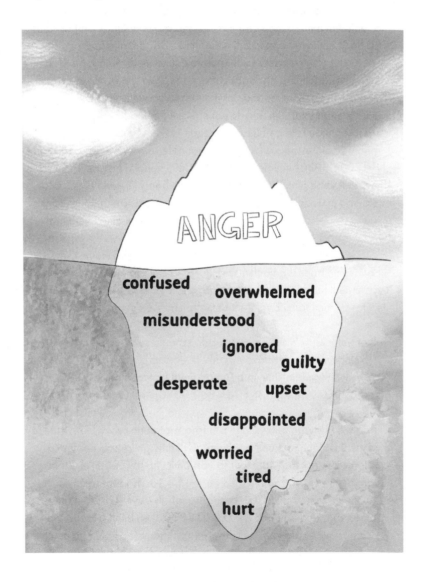

And then there is our threshold – the point at which we bubble over. When we are going through settled times, it can be easier to cope with smaller things, but when we have been stressed and distressed, sometimes the slightest thing can push us over the edge and lead to a big reaction from us. We can think about our feelings as a fizzy drink inside a bottle that we carry around. When we are having an easier time, our fizzy drinks bottle can sit comfortably without being shaken up much. But when we are stressed, distressed and having a harder time, our drinks bottle gets shaken up a lot and so it doesn't take much for the liquid inside to fizz out the moment something triggers our lid to come loose. Grief is likely to give your bottle a lot of opportunities to get shaken up until it explodes (sometimes spectacularly).

That doesn't mean, of course, that we want to go around exploding at people or in places. We'll come to what to do about angry feelings in a while, but let's spend a little longer trying to understand your anger first.

OLIVIA'S PERSONAL EXPERIENCE

The hard part about grief is that it can make our emotions confusing. I remember being sad about losing a piece of jewellery a few months after my dad died, and I was so sad looking for it in my room, around the house. And eventually, when I still couldn't find it, I just became so angry and frustrated, and my sadness sort of developed into more feelings.

Talking to a friend or family member and explaining to

them how I felt always helped, and afterwards I was often able to laugh about how frustrated or angry I had become about something that I didn't need to. Our emotions during grief are all contorted and stretched out of shape, because they're being used so much more and in more direct ways, focusing on that loss and the process of grief. It's okay to feel all out of sorts and recognize that you might not usually react like this.

There are all kinds of reasons why we feel angry after someone died. It might be because of what happened when they died, feelings of anger left over from while they were alive, or anger at situations you are now facing. Your anger can be directed at different people and triggered by different situations. Do any of these make sense to you?

- **Feeling angry at others.** Perhaps specific people in your life make you feel angry, or maybe it just feels as though everyone is really annoying. Feeling misunderstood can lead to being cross with people as they do not *get* what you are going through. You might feel hurt that people are not supporting you as you had hoped they would and aren't getting how hard life is right now. Sometimes as people try to step in to help, they won't always get it right and that can be hard. They might assume how you are feeling or take on roles that the person who died did. That can be really painful...and frustrating. For people closest to you, maybe they too are trying to manage grief and you just keep setting each other off.
- **Feeling angry about the person who died.** There may be unresolved things that you are carrying –

small ones like when they took your phone away because you hadn't done a chore, or bigger ones such as difficult things in your relationship with them. You might also be angry because they are not here to help you with practical things like homework or taking you to a club or because they have left you to deal with this grief (even when they didn't choose to die). If the person ended their own life, then there could be a whole lot of things to be angry about (there's a bit about this in Chapter 1 on complications and traumatic deaths).

- **Feeling angry at yourself.** Sometimes when you feel as if you are not handling things as well as you think you should, then you might direct your anger at yourself. Sometimes feeling angry with yourself can go hand in hand with feeling cross with the person who died, especially if you feel a bit guilty that you are angry with them.

But you are more than your grief, and not everything you feel is because of your grief. Stuff will sometimes just wind you up because it *is* annoying. And then it will be even more annoying if everyone assumes it's because your person died.

OLIVIA'S PERSONAL EXPERIENCE

I always felt a lot of anger when I was very early into the grief process. Even things that you wouldn't think would make someone angry. But for me, I get overwhelmed and frustrated very easily, and anger sort of just erupts from that. Lots of adults in my life were also memorably angry and frustrated when I was younger, so it was almost a comfort emotion to me; when I get sad, I associate it with frustration and anger. But I recognized that I couldn't do that every time I was sad – I'd have been angry constantly! I found people I could trust to talk to about these feelings and I was able to work out ways that helped me recognize when I was feeling these ways and how I could deal with it before it became too much for me.

Making sense of your anger

Let's spend a moment to think about the last few times you felt angry:

1. What was happening that triggered your anger?
2. What did you do with your anger?
3. What happened afterwards as a consequence of your anger?

Chi spent time thinking about the last time she had felt angry:

1. My brother had just said mean things about my friend who died by suicide.
2. I shouted at my brother and smashed a plate.
3. My dad said I would have to do the dishwasher for a week.

We think that young people are sometimes treated a bit unfairly for being angry. When your amygdala triggers a *flight* or *freeze* response instead of a *fight* response, people are more likely to see you as feeling sad or fearful, and this tends to prompt a kinder response from them – often they want to help you. When people see a fight response, an angry outburst instead, you don't always get such a helpful response. In fact, sometimes other people get cross with you, and the situation escalates further. That doesn't mean that we should be able to do anything we like with our anger and get away with it because we're grieving. It is important that we express angry feelings without anyone or anything getting hurt and without getting into trouble. It's just that anger itself isn't a bad feeling – it is just your brain detecting a potential threat. Feeling angry might even be totally appropriate for the situation. This section isn't about telling you not to get so angry, but about helping you with ideas about what to do to make things less hard for you. Here's an idea you could try in the moment when you are getting angry.

What to do to cope with your anger

STEP 1 – NOTICE THE FEELING
Can you notice when your anger has been triggered? What clues does your body give you? Noticing these is a key first step in understanding what might be about to happen.

STEP 2 – NAME THE FEELING
Can you name the exact feeling and why you think it's been triggered? For example: 'I'm feeling really frustrated that my brother could be so mean and hurt me like that.'

STEP 3 – NUMBER THE STRENGTH
Can you give this feeling a number to show the strength of it? For example, is it a 7 out of 10? Pretty strong but not out of control?

STEP 4 – NOW PLAN YOUR RESPONSE

The thing about these first three steps is that they give you a little pause and encourage your smart brain to do some thinking (working out physical clues, naming the emotion and rating it) rather than your amygdala just reacting. This can interrupt your anger response, giving you a moment to decide what to do with your anger that won't hurt you or anyone else and won't get you into trouble.

All this looks pretty straightforward when you read it (we hope!), but you probably know that it's not so easy to follow in the moment, when your anger is already triggered. Work on practising Step 1 for a bit and then gradually add the next step in and the next.

When it comes to Step 4, you will find it easier to come up with options for what to do with your anger in advance when you're feeling calm and settled. Make a list of possible responses that would help you express yourself and calm yourself down but in ways that won't make things worse.

Young people have told us they sometimes try:

- listening to music – some have a special playlist that first matches their mood and then helps change it
- doing something physical such as sit-ups, bouncing a ball, squeezing their pillow, dancing to their favourite track
- scrunching up newspaper – some like to write down what they are cross about on it first and then rip it or screw it up
- telling someone, even if it's just themselves – it can be

really helpful to be able to put those strong feelings into words and feel listened to

- getting out into the fresh air – sometimes a change of environment can help trigger a change in direction of their mood, giving them something different to focus on
- being with someone (it might be a pet) who can give them a big hug, but not ask or expect them to say what is going on.

OLIVIA'S PERSONAL EXPERIENCE

A big coping mechanism for me was long-distance running with headphones in. Music that I liked or felt matched my mood, and running until I felt tired, usually meant my anger had dwindled, too. It was very accessible to me, and I looked forward to it most days after school. Even if I hadn't been angry that day, I realized I could keep on top of my feelings and feel better before the anger had even built up.

Do any of these work for you? Can you add to this list?

Social support

We have talked often about the value of social support; this can be really important to help you manage anger, too. People whom you trust can support you with any or all of the steps above (notice, name, number and now plan your response). People you live with might be good at helping you notice when those anger clues are just starting. If they know what you're handling and what you are trying to do, you will have someone who can coach you through it until you feel ready to follow it on your own. This could include a friend when you're out and about, and maybe an adult at school who has helped you plan your options if anger gets triggered there. Remember that others won't know what's on your mind and what's hard right now if you don't tell them. So they won't have a chance to understand and try to support you. If you can, try to tell key people. This includes telling them how best to support you and what really doesn't help.

When you might need more help

Sometimes feeling cross and angry a lot means you start doing things that are pretty serious. This could cause a lot of problems for you in school, at home, with peers. If this is the case, you might need a bit more help.

PAST TRAUMA OR TRAUMA BECAUSE OF THE DEATH

If you've experienced a lot of difficult traumatic things, then your brain might have adapted to be triggered to fight, flight or freeze more quickly. This means that you find distressing thoughts and images keep coming into your mind and make you feel as if the trauma is happening all over again. Because it's really unpleasant when this happens, you try really hard to avoid things that could be upsetting. Dealing with all this is very hard, and these traumatic experiences can leave you on high alert even after the danger has passed. This can make you irritable and grumpy quite a lot, with your emotions ready to fizz over really quickly with only the slightest trigger.

If you find that your responses are frequently really big and are putting you or others at risk or putting important relationships under more strain, then you might need extra help (see Chapter 3).

Ideas for coping with worries and fear

As if sadness and anger weren't enough to be contending with, struggling with fear and worry are pretty common following a death. Maybe you were always a bit of a worrier and now that you are grieving you find that your worries have gone up several gears. Or maybe this is a newer experience for you and the loss of your person has triggered an uncomfortable level of fear. A number of neurodivergent young people have told us that this is something they find especially hard.

If fear and worry are something you've always struggled with, it could be helpful to think about why. The evidence suggests that this can be partly down to our genes, in the same way as we inherit eye colour or hair colour. If you have worked out that you are not the only person in your family who tends to get anxious, this could be part of the reason. We also know that being around other people who worry a lot or are scared of things models worrying for us, so that we start to see the world from an anxious point of view. Maybe you have noticed that some of your worries and fears aren't that different to those of the people who brought you up. And then, of course, life events can trigger a lot of worry and fear, and this is pretty justified. If someone has died, that alone can start or make fears and worries harder to manage.

Maybe your home has become a place of worry right now; with so many of you grieving, it can be easy for worries and fears to become almost *contagious* as everyone's anxiety goes up a gear. Noticing that this is happening is a good first step, and then you can use some of the strategies we describe here to start to make a dent in the fear and give you some control. Encourage others in your household to try some of them too.

In this section, we'll unpick why fears and worries seem to be a part of grief for many young people, and then we'll offer some ideas for you to try.

Let's start with fears

We've already talked about the fight, flight, freeze response and how it can trigger us into big outbursts of anger and frustration. The same goes with fear. We need our brains to be alert to danger because that's what helps us to get to safety when there is a real threat. The trouble with anxiety is that it *assumes* a threat is dangerous rather than working out if it actually is.

It's a bit like a smoke alarm. We need it to help us detect if there is smoke, but it can't tell the difference between a bit of burnt toast and an actual fire. When it goes off, we need to work out what the threat is and decide on an appropriate course of action. If, at the first sound of the smoke alarm, we always evacuated our properties and called for the fire service before checking if it is only toast, we would likely be unpopular. Of course, if an actual fire had started, we would need to do exactly that. With the burnt toast, where there is no actual danger – we just need to open the windows and waft a tea towel to create a bit of breeze to help the smoke alarm stop beeping.

But it can be really difficult to work out if a threat is real or not when our bodies are in a state of anxiety. Our chest might be pounding, our limbs shaking, our stomach full of butterflies and our mind only able to focus on getting away from the potential danger. Just when we need our smart thinking brain to help us out, we are driven by fear instead.

So why does grief often buddy up with fear?

When your person died, this might have been such a shock or so traumatic and distressing that it triggered a strong and totally understandable fear response from you. Even now that the event has passed, your body and mind are still on high alert, waiting for something else bad to happen. This is not your fault; it's just the way you experienced their death and the way your body and mind are holding on to it. You might now be fearful of things that remind you of the death and want to avoid going near those triggers, or even thinking about them.

66 After Dad died, I found I couldn't face going to his room because that's where the paramedics had been when they tried to save him. Every time I even went to that part of the landing, I would feel the same fear and panic I had felt then. (Tara)

66 When my baby brother Jamil died before he was born, I couldn't stop being scared that something else bad would happen. Going to my nan's was hard because that's where I was when

I heard that Mum was in hospital. And I've found it really hard to be with my new baby cousin as I'm scared something will happen to him too, so I usually make excuses and say I have too much homework to do. (Kareem)

Staying away from things that make you feel anxious can feel like a good idea in the short term. But in the long term, it doesn't work out so well. It just keeps the fear going and stops you from believing you can cope with hard things. Which is not really true as you are working hard to cope with grief every single day.

Death is also out of our control, which is a bit of a problem because as humans we often feel safer when we are in control. Fear then tries to 'help us out' by putting some control back in by giving us rules about what is safe and certain. It tells us that doing or not doing things in a certain way will make everyone safe. Of course, we know that we can't control everything around us, but fear can make it feel that way. Sometimes we even develop some habits or routines that fear tells us are crucial to stop more bad things from happening.

66 After my cousin Ethan died, my uncle gave me his keyring and said for me to look after it and that it would help me feel close to Ethan. At first, I kept it in my trouser pocket and would put it in my palm to help me remember him and then leave it by my bed at night. But as the months passed, I found I had to keep squeezing the keyring all the time to stop me forgetting Ethan. This kept going, so now I must squeeze it three times every hour including throughout the night. (Yasmin)

If this is happening for you, tell someone who can support you in getting the help you need (see Chapter 3).

Starting to face your fears

There is a lot you can do to help manage your fears. The first thing is to recognize when you are becoming anxious by spotting the signs in your body. Where does it start for you? Head? Chest? Limbs? Stomach? Remembering that these are normal responses is helpful as then you'll know you don't need to be scared of feeling scared.

If your fear is stopping you from doing things, the next thing will be to make a plan to face those fears. As we mentioned earlier, in the short term, avoiding the thing that you fear is usually easier, but by facing your fears you can find that they are often not as difficult as you think, and that you can cope. This might be easy to say, but it might feel pretty difficult to do.

To help with this, it can be worth thinking about all the reasons to face your fears to give you some motivation to get started.

Let's use Tara from above as an example. She found she couldn't go back into her parents' bedroom after her dad died in there and the memory of the paramedics trying to treat him was so overwhelming. She made a list of all the reasons why she wanted to face her fear:

1. So I can go in and snuggle with Mum if I've had a bad dream.

2. So I can watch Sunday morning TV with Mum and our dog Cocoa again.
3. So I can be with Mum if she's feeling lonely.
4. So I can feel close to Dad (and the memories of him snoring!).
5. So I can feel brave again.

Have a go at making your own list (you don't need to fill it all in – you might just have one or two reasons that are important to you):

1. . . . .

. . . .

2. . . . .

. . . .

3. . . . .

. . . .

4. . . . .

. . . .

5. . . . .

. . . .

If we were to ask Tara to simply go into her parents' bedroom and sit on the bed, even the thought of it might feel too overwhelming, so she might not even try. Instead, Tara sets out some mini steps towards her overall goals of being in the room or snuggling in the bed.

She writes them on her step-by-step plan working her way up from the bottom:

Ultimate goal: Watch TV from Mum and Dad's bed

Step 7: Go and sit on the bed on my own

Step 6: Go and sit on the bed with Mum

Step 5: Go and touch the bed and look around the bedroom

Step 4: Go into the bedroom on my own without Mum being there

Step 3: Take a step into the bedroom and chat to Mum

Step 2: Open the bedroom door and chat to Mum

Step 1: Go and stand by the bedroom door and talk to Mum

Tara found that starting Step 1 and 2 wasn't as hard as she had expected, but she had to repeat Step 3 several times. She also knew that she had to stay in her parents' room for long enough that her fear reduced and her body got used to it. Over the next few weeks, she kept working on her plan. Sometimes it wasn't easy and she got a bit tearful, but it didn't take too long for her to feel comfortable in the room again.

Over to you!

Can you make a step-by-step plan using the list you just created for motivation?

You don't need to have six or seven steps – you might find you only need three or four, or perhaps need ten or more. It's better to keep the steps small and achievable – it's much easier to whizz through a few steps in one go than it is to get stuck halfway through a really big step. Remember to keep trying and to stay with each step until it doesn't make you feel so fearful.

Ultimate goal:

....

....

↑

Step 6:

....

....

↑

Step 5:

....

....

↑

Step 4:

....

....

↑

Step 3:

....

....

↑

Step 2:

....

....

↑

Step 1:

....

....

Two more tips:

1. Don't feel you need to do it all alone. Having the support of someone you trust can help – Tara had her mum for company for some of the steps – might be an important part of the plan.
2. Reward yourself – it's okay to build in rewards as you make progress on your plan. Talk about these with someone who can support you – or, even better, provide the rewards!

Evidence for your fears

Sometimes fears need a different approach: when it's not that you are avoiding the fear, but the problem is more about the way it plays tricks on your mind. It might make you feel that something bad is just about to happen all the time. This is what it was like for Kareem when his baby brother Jamil was stillborn and he had a constant fear about something else bad happening. It wasn't that he could really face this fear – it was just in his head. But realizing that anxiety isn't always truthful, accurate or helpful was an important step. Kareem started to work out the evidence for the things anxiety was telling him. He did this by *putting the thought in court*. In a court in the UK, there would be lawyers for and against a case, each putting forward evidence about whether the person on trial did commit the crime. When putting the thought in court, you are trying to think through carefully whether there is evidence for and against the fear you have.

The thought

'Something bad will happen to the others in my family'

Evidence for this thought	Evidence against this thought
• My baby brother died • Everyone dies • Bad things always happen to me	• Of all the people in my family, Jamil is the only one to die • I've been alive for 14 years 3 months (approximately 5200 days) and nobody else in my family has died • Jamil dying was a truly bad and sad thing, but some okay things and some good things have also happened

Of course, there may be evidence for the anxiety, but there may also be evidence that weakens the case. And this can help us find some more balanced thoughts and not just listen to the anxious ones. You don't have to 'get rid' of your anxious thoughts – there are often understandable reasons for them – but also knowing there is some evidence against them can help you get more of a grip on your fears instead of them controlling you. Give it a try and test out the evidence for a fear that's been on your mind.

Working on worries

For some young people, worrying can become a way of life, especially after a death. To be fair, there can be plenty to occupy your mind including practical, financial and emotional aspects. Jared, for example, worried about:

❝ How will I get to rugby training now?

❝ Will we have enough money to stay living here with my aunt?

❝ How is my aunt going to keep everything going on her own now?

❝ What if something happens to my aunt too? Then where will I live?

Constant worrying is hard and it can really get in the way of enjoying your teenage years. It's like walking around with an umbrella all the time waiting for it to rain. That's helpful to a degree but might get in the way of doing other things if you've always got one hand keeping your umbrella up. And if your mind is constantly focusing on the weather, watching out for rain clouds, then having the time or energy to concentrate on other things might be difficult.

Sorting out your worries

One thing that can help is to sort out your worries into categories to work out what or who they are about. This might include worries about your:

- family
- friends
- school/college
- health
- future.

Setting things out like this can help you see whether there are lots of worries in one section or whether your worries spread over several categories.

You can then try to work out exactly what each worry is about, not just the theme of it.

For example, Jared worried that:

66 My aunt isn't coping as I hear her crying on the phone to her girlfriend. My friends are laughing about me behind my back. I'm not going to get the grades I need to get to college or uni. I will get a tumour like my dad and have to go through all that awful treatment he did. There won't be jobs for us in the future as the world is so rubbish right now.

Worries you can't change
Some of these worries are the kind of things that many young people might worry about, but there is actually nothing that you can do about it. It is not usually possible to just stop worrying or stop thinking about it – the more you try to stop thinking about something, the more it comes into your mind.

Talking back to the worry
So instead of getting too stressed when the worries come into your mind, give them a neutral hello (don't be too friendly), let them say what they want to say and then remind them it's out of your control so there's no point them hanging around. A bit like this:

- Ah, it's you again. So 'good' of you to drop by [sarcasm required]. You're here to remind me about getting a brain tumour. Now, you and I know I can't do anything about that worry so you might as well move on. I've got other stuff to do.

And then you need to be strict with yourself and actually do something else that shifts your attention, rather than giving the worry any more of your time.

Make a list of activities that use up a lot of your attention so that the time flies. If your worries are really stubborn, then you will need to work on things that *really* need your concentration so that there is no room for worrying as you are totally consumed in them for a while.

These might include:

- fitness exercises
- reading
- computer games
- helping others
- designing things – your future home/car/AI product
- craft activities
- puzzles
- number games
- movies
- making your own vlog.

You could also put the thought in court for some of these worries, as we explained above. See if you can work out the evidence for the worry being accurate and true. For example, if you are worried about your friends laughing behind your back, you could work out the evidence for and against that being true.

Postponing the worry

Have you ever had someone delay an appointment you had with them? Maybe you've arranged to see a teacher at lunch break, and they've apologized and said that they can no longer see you then but they could at 4 p.m. So you go back at 4 p.m. You could do the same to your worries. When they crop up at an inconvenient time, you could agree that you will worry about them, but not just now. You can make a time to do the worrying. You can then go about your day knowing that you don't need to worry about the worries just now, because you're going to do that later. Sometimes, when the allotted time comes around, your worries don't even show up. But if they do, you can focus on them, perhaps using some of the other strategies discussed here. It means that you are able to reduce the amount that the worry is affecting you and your life.

Problem solving

But sometimes there are things that you can do about a worry if it is actually a realistic one. If this is the case, try some problem solving. This is about working out what you can do, what's in your control. This won't necessarily stop the thing from happening, but it's about finding ways you can begin to cope with it, or at least working out what your options are.

This might work well for the worry about getting the grades to get to college or uni as it will help you get started on some action to help with your studies – if you do some problem solving with it. What are your options?

- Find out what your predicted grades are.
- Find out what grades you need for college or uni.
- Find out how you can improve your grades with extra work or study.
- Make a plan to do some extra work.
- Work out what else you could do if your grades aren't quite high enough.

There are a lot of options to help towards reducing this worry – putting you back in control of how you respond to this problem. Some of these options will be things you can do immediately, but others are things you need to put on hold and come back to later, like postponing the worry. Getting busy with things that help you change the focus of your attention meanwhile will help you manage so the worry doesn't have too tight a grip on you right now.

Other people's worries

Of course, there are some worries that will really benefit from communication, particularly those that involve other people such as Jared's worry about how his aunt was coping. When Jared found the courage to talk to his aunt, and explain how he worried about her, his aunt was able to share that she finds it helpful to have a cry to her girlfriend, to let her feelings out as she is grieving for the death of Jared's dad, her brother.

Jared's aunt was then able to explain that although she doesn't know exactly how things will work out, she is absolutely determined to be the best aunt that she can to

Jared and to look after him not only while he is growing up, but as an adult as well. She also reminded him that he can always come to her if he is worried so they can see what they can work out together. This worry felt far less powerful once he had shared it with his aunt.

Worrying about more death

Worrying about dying is really common after someone has died, whether it is a fear of other people dying or of yourself dying. This makes sense. If your world has just been shattered by someone significant to you dying, then it's completely understandable that you worry (a lot) that death is going to come visiting again. Some people around you might make all sorts of promises to you about this. While they mean well and want to reassure you, no one can really promise that no one else will die, because everyone will die, one day.

What we can work out, however, is whether it is *likely* that others in your life will die soon. Quite a number of young people are affected by bereavement – in the UK, about 46,000 children and young people experience the death of a parent each year. But very, very few experience the death of both parents. Some families do have genetic conditions or illnesses that can affect life span, but most families do not. Most deaths that occur in the lives of young people are from illnesses or accidents, and these tend to be quite random rather than likely to happen again.

So we won't make unfounded guarantees that this will not happen to you again. Instead, let's give a little bit of attention to how you would cope if, very sadly, another death does happen. With good care and support, young people do cope, and you would find ways, too. We've met and worked with young people who have been through immense tragedy, and it's not been easy for them. Before the deaths, they didn't know how they would cope, but step by step, day by day, they did cope and they still do.

Let's try to see which strategies we looked at earlier might be helpful with this kind of worry about other people dying.

- Talking back to the worry – letting it come into your mind but telling it what you think and not giving it too much attention.
- Giving something else your attention – choose an activity that you get absorbed in.
- Problem solving to work out any options that you might have.
- Communicating with others so you can be supported by them – this might include finding out what the plan is if the person looking after you was to die.

Worry decision tree

When you're not sure straight away which worry strategy to try, you could use the worry decision tree here to help you find a way.

NOTICE THE WORRY

What am I worried about?

Can I do something about it?

No — Let the worry go → Change focus of attention

Yes — Make a plan: What, How, When?

Now? — Do it → Let the worry go → Change focus of attention

Later? — Schedule it → Let the worry go → Change focus of attention

OLIVIA'S PERSONAL EXPERIENCE

Fears after someone has died can manifest in very different ways. I was never fearful of how my dad died, because it wasn't an accident or illness (something out of his control). But I became fearful of what would happen as life continued. Would just Mum working be enough to pay the bills and buy food? Would I feel this sad forever? Would all this trauma affect how I did in my exams? Would I ever be able to listen to certain songs my dad liked again? Would I ever be able to go back to the place his death occurred?

Some of these were things I shouldn't have been worrying about as a 13-year-old grieving a fresh loss, but your mind doesn't rationalize like that. Some of those worries, I have worked through and beaten, years later, and others I found too hard and are still worries that I have. But they don't take up as much space in my mind as they used to, and as I've grown around my grief, I realize which fears I can control and which fears I can't control, and that helps me to decide whether they're worth my worry and time to work through them or not.

Even if the worries sound crazy and silly to you, they come from somewhere, and it's always worth talking to someone you trust about them, so you can make plans to work through them and stop them being worries in your mind. Someone without that worry might be better at helping you see how to approach it, and that could be really helpful.

Ideas for coping with school and peers

Returning to school or college

Returning to school or college after someone has died is a big step. Sometimes you might welcome the chance to get out of your home and have a break from the grief there. It might also give you the opportunity to think about something else, even if it's only a physics assessment. And you can have some time with your friends.

Doing all this doesn't mean you have forgotten about your grief or the person who died. It just means you have been able to step away from the intense feelings and benefit from doing something else that gives you a bit of routine and feels a little bit like normal.

However, going back to school isn't always straightforward or easy. If you have not been involved in decision making about returning to school, that can be hard, because a lot of things already feel out of your control after someone has died. You might be under pressure from adults who think you should return before you're ready to or think you ought to stay at home for longer than you want to.

Planning your return

If it is possible to discuss and plan your return, this can help you feel more in control and help those around you, both at home and at school or college, to support you better. Very often, adults, typically your parents or carers, will take the lead in telling your school that someone important has died. It is best if you can be included in what is shared and what is kept private. Sometimes young people don't want anyone to know that someone has died as it feels too raw, and they don't want to be questioned about what happened or how they are doing. This is totally understandable.

In the long term, though, that is unlikely to be helpful. When no one knows what has happened, this can make your experience at school pretty lonely, and no one will know how to support you or why you might be finding things harder. This makes things really tricky as you carry your grief alone throughout the school day. It is totally fine, however, to decide what the adults at school can be told. You might feel ready to build on this in the weeks that follow, explaining a bit more to the adults you trust.

You may have already returned to school some weeks or months ago. Maybe your friends, classmates and adults in school have been good at supporting you. However, if you've been keeping everything very private so far, you might want to consider the ideas about letting others know so that they can look out for you.

We know that grief doesn't go away after the first weeks and months, but not everyone around you at school or college will understand that. They might think that if you 'look okay' after a while, it's all fine now. But when you've been bereaved, it can be helpful to have people to support you throughout your school or college years.

It may be helpful for you to outline how you would and wouldn't like to be supported. So if you don't want to be asked how you are feeling by all your teachers, that's okay.

They may still want to check in with you – in fact, we would hope that staff at your school will check in with you. Not so they ask you lots of questions or expect you to tell them stuff you're not ready to talk about, but to show that they care about how you are doing.

You might agree a plan for who checks in with you and when, so you are not caught by surprise in the corridor when you least expect it. Staff might want to know if there is anything they can do to support you. You might have a clear idea – for example, having an exit pass to use if you feel overwhelmed and need a short break from your lesson. Or they can tell you about places you can go if you need to be quiet for a while or how you can get support from your student or pastoral manager if you'd like to.

If school or college feels overwhelming, talk with those you live with and your school about whether you could attend part-time – even for the first week or so – and plan how you can gradually increase your attendance to full-time. Schools want their pupils in all the time, of course, but they will often be open to having you in some of the time rather than not at all – especially if they can see you are making an effort to attend. Some of the ideas in the section on worries and fears might be helpful if you are feeling anxious about being back in school.

OLIVIA'S PERSONAL EXPERIENCE

I really struggled going back to school after my dad died. My teachers had all been told, but none of them really knew how to approach me and no one let me know who I could talk to or where I could go when I was overwhelmed. My first class was English, and our teacher had us reading a poem. The poem was about a child whose dad had just died. I remember being very upset and angry that my teacher hadn't warned me or changed the poem, because she knew that I had just lost my dad. And I felt very upset because I didn't want to draw attention to myself in front of my friends and peers by asking her to change it, because I wasn't ready to talk about what had happened yet.

Instead, I burst into tears and ran out into the hallway, with my teacher following me out. I told her how shocked I was at the poem and asked her why she hadn't warned me, and she told me I could skip the class and go into the library until my next lesson. I waited, crying, in the hallway until another teacher came to walk me over, and by this time lots of attention had been drawn to me, which made me feel worse on top of the grief and sadness. I had a lot of times for the next few years where my school didn't support me, and it was hard to find adults I could talk to who had the right training or even understanding. I turned to my mum a lot because I didn't have an outlet at school, which was isolating.

Telling your friends and classmates

Some of the same things will apply to telling your friends and classmates about your bereavement. You are under no obligation to tell people, but very often the news that someone has died does become known and shared around school anyway. If you have taken the lead in letting your friends know and maybe asking your form tutor to tell your class, then at least you had some control over what was shared and whether you were there when the news was shared. Sometimes we can feel so private about difficult events in our lives that we can't bear the thought of people knowing. We can't guarantee that everyone will be brilliant at supporting you, but if they don't know, there's a pretty high chance that someone will say something unknowingly, and that can be really painful to hear and handle on your own.

We hope you have a best friend or maybe a group of friends who are great at supporting you (and maybe pretty good at baking muffins on demand or going easy when you're playing games online!). The reality is that good friends will try to be good friends to you, but they probably won't always get it right. They won't always say the right thing and won't always realize if you're having a bad time on a particular day. If they're trying and actually care about you, then that's a pretty good start.

You can help them a bit by telling them what helps you and what is annoying. Tell them when you're feeling sad or grumpy, and they'll have a better chance of getting more things right for you next time. Some young people have told us that messaging friends on their phone sometimes feels a bit easier to do because you can communicate at a time and in a space that feels safer, helping you to be honest about how you're doing.

OLIVIA'S PERSONAL EXPERIENCE

Lots of people I went to school with knew that I had lost my dad, and so no one was really surprised that I was quite down for a while afterwards. But some days, my sadness or grumpy face was just because I was tired or hated maths class – it wasn't necessarily because I was actively grieving in that moment. And I would tell my friends and family this, because (a) it helped me feel less sad and grumpy and (b) it was a distraction from all the other sadness – and eventually I could laugh with my friends about how much I hated maths. But if you don't communicate with people, they might give you space because they think you need it to grieve, when it might be the last thing you want at that moment.

You may have a friend who is grieving, too. Checking in with them might be really useful – there may be ways of supporting each other. Starting spontaneous conversations at school is not always so easy, whether in geography lessons or the lunch queue. It can be pretty hard to bring up your grief and their grief, but the conversations that you have could be really valuable. Maybe it's just knowing that someone else gets this grief thing – even if it's just a look that you share between you.

Having your friends as friends

Friends are mostly good at friendship stuff – that's why you became buddies/pals/mates/friends. Your friends probably won't be ideal as your therapists, but they might be good listeners or good at lifting your mood, getting you out, distracting you from your grief by having a laugh or even by taking the mickey out of you. It's good to have some things that feel a bit normal when so much of your life feels far from normal.

And if they're struggling to know how to be your friend because they're worried about saying or doing the wrong thing and upsetting you, then, if you can, give them a bit of guidance and try to work it out together. Tell them you're okay about them mentioning their dads, but you hope they'll understand if sometimes you're sad that your dad isn't around. If they're good friends, they're probably worth sticking with, even if they are a bit rubbish at the grief stuff.

When others aren't so friendly

We hope you don't have to face people being mean about what you have been through, but young people we have worked with tell us it does happen. Sometimes, classmates are accidentally insensitive because they haven't stopped to think about how massive and intensely painful it is when someone important dies. Others sometimes deliberately set out to cause more pain by repeatedly making fun of your grief or saying things to disrespect the person who died. This isn't okay. You shouldn't have to put up with anyone doing this.

Schools and colleges haven't got perfect ways to stop mean things from happening, but if they don't even know about it, they can't put things in place to back you up. Use the adults you have good relationships with to help support you. And if you are at risk of retaliating and hurting the person who was mean, ask for help so that you don't end up getting into trouble yourself. This seems pretty unfair, but hurting others doesn't make anything better or easier for us. Often things become even more complicated.

When your friend has died

When your friend has died, then school, rather than being an escape from the grief at home, will be where your pain feels hardest. You might miss the lessons, breaktimes, journey to or from school, and the school day can become a tough reminder of everything you shared and everything that is now missing. That's really tough.

We hope that there are others around at school who get it, so you don't feel so alone. Having a group to share memories and help get through it together can be a powerful thing. However, your relationship with your friend was unique between you, and the things you shared and now missed are unique too, so it's okay if you are grieving differently to the rest of your friendship group.

Using your support team to help you cope with school

Even our favourite people aren't usually good at everything, nor would we necessarily want them to be. But we can find that the relationships we have support us in different ways. Have a think about who is in your support team to help you cope with school. Some people are good to talk to, others to cheer you on, some will be company you can be honest and cry with, some will be useful at helping you in practical ways, or giving you a much-needed hug or making you laugh. Hopefully, across your back-up team there are people who fulfil all these roles and help you feel supported in different ways.

Learning to learn again

Grieving is hard work. It takes up a lot of energy and attention. So it's not that surprising that your bereavement can make concentrating, learning and being motivated to participate in lessons a lot more challenging. Many young people have told us that the quiet time in lessons, when their teacher was giving a long explanation about something (even if it was quite interesting), was one of the hardest times.

Perhaps it's just hard to focus and give the lesson your attention and your mind wanders. Maybe this is the time when your most painful memories and worries about the future take over your brain. You might not feel so interested and motivated to learn right now. Other things are your priority. This all makes sense to us.

For many young people, given a bit of time and kind support from staff and classmates, you will gradually find your concentration improves and you do catch up. If it is hard to feel motivated right now, then that's understandable – losing your sister, your best friend or your beloved nan might feel like the only thing in the universe that is worth bothering about. Some teenagers have told us that even though it was hard, they found more motivation after their person died. They wanted to achieve well to make them proud, wanted to honour their memory or follow in a similar field of study. It took time, and a lot of effort, but many of those young people blew everyone away with their efforts, in spite of the many challenges they were facing.

If you find that even after many months, concentrating is still really hard and those painful memories are still regular visitors to your mind, it might be worth getting a bit of help. This may be one of the ways the trauma of what happened is affecting you. Letting adults know this is still happening is important. Then they can support you, rather than get on your case for not completing your work.

If your teachers know, they can also look out for signs that you are having a hard time in lessons. They can then gently refocus you, helping to take your mind away from distressing thoughts. They will also be more understanding if you need to use things to help with concentration – for example, things to fidget with or doodle on to help focus or calm you down. This tends to work best when you have discussed it with adults in school so that the strategies to help you refocus are agreed.

Managing all this can make you more irritable as we talked about in the section on coping with anger. Again, letting adults know means they can set up systems that help you spot when your frustration is building and offer you some time out or other support that you choose. You will still have to follow the rules and boundaries of your school or college, but hopefully they can show some understanding about why it is so hard right now and why talking it through together might really help.

Triggers in school

Reminders of death can occur at any time – switching on the TV, people making jokes, a story or memory appearing on your phone, seeing newspaper headlines are just a few. School or college can be another place where reminders seem relentless. The curriculum at school is littered with topics that might be hard for you after someone has died.

In English, it seems that nearly every author likes to include topics about loss and death. In science, topics about the heart or cancer or something else linked with what happened to your person can be frequently covered. History lessons often focus on war and conflict, which can be really painful if your home country was caught up in a war or if the person you are grieving for died in the military services. PSHE, of course, covers many sensitive topics including mental health and suicide. Loads of subjects might have content that reminds you of your loss, and even if the topic doesn't arise, there might be something else about the lesson that is a reminder. For example, maybe your mum always helped you with maths homework, or perhaps your older sister was a brilliant chemist so chemistry always brings her to mind.

Young people have told us that it really helps to be given advance notice of a topic or lesson. Part of this is because it gives them a chance to work out how they feel about it and if they might need extra support. They have also said that they felt really supported by their teacher who remembered and thought of them. They have also told us that sometimes the lead-up to the lesson made them feel a bit (or a lot) nervous, but when it came to it, they felt okay.

" I knew that in the summer term we would be studying *Romeo and Juliet*, and even though I didn't know much about the story, I did know that it involved suicide. I started to spend a lot of time thinking about how I would cope, and a lot of memories of my brother who had taken his own life kept coming back. I was starting to panic about going to English lessons, even though we hadn't even started reading it. In the end, I spoke to my student manager, and he helped me talk to my teacher.

I could tell that my teacher wasn't sure how to help or what to say or not say. But between us all, we agreed that I would not be asked to read out loud or give my opinion unless I wanted to. I could also use my exit pass at any point, and because my teacher knew why I might need time out, she would not ask me to explain. I was also allowed to sit next to my best friend in those lessons, which made me feel safer as she knew what I'd been through. (Conor)

And it's not just lessons. Events in school, such as charity events or memorials, can be acute reminders of your experience of grief. This is all really tough and may present lots of additional challenges. No one can really give you an 'opt out just in case' card. If they did, you might end up missing large parts of your school life just in case something was upsetting.

These are things that make managing all this just a little less hard:

- Keeping a conversation going with adults at school will be helpful. Ask someone from home or one of your friends to support you with this if you need it. They may not know how you are doing if you don't say, even just a little bit.
- Ask staff to let you know if a related topic will be coming up in future lessons so at least you have a bit of time to prepare yourself.
- Work together to agree on how you can be supported when a difficult topic comes up. Could there be an agreement that you can take some time out if you need it?

- Ask a student manager to keep staff updated as you move up through the school so that new staff are made aware of sensitive topics for you.
- At times, staff won't remember or realize the importance of warning you about topics. We hope you develop skills to help you cope with this unpredictability and have good support around you when it happens.

Moving on to a new school or college

Changing school or college as part of a usual transition (to sixth form, for example) can be an additional challenge. Sometimes young people have to change the school they attend during the school year. This might be one of the changes that had to happen after the death of your person. In that case, it would have been a change that was out of your control. Starting a new school or college means having to start again with friendships, getting to know new teachers and working out what to do with your grief – who to tell and when and how. It's your choice, but as we discussed earlier, if no one knows, no one can support you.

You as the expert in bereavement

Although it wasn't a role you chose, as you find ways to cope with the hurt of your grief, you become an expert by experience. And maybe one day you'll be able to use your experience to help others really understand these topics. You might also be able to talk to staff about how your school could set up support for bereaved young people – if they don't already do this. How could you make things better for other bereaved students who start at your school or college? What does your school need to know and be able to do?

What support would be helpful – maybe new ideas that are a better 'fit' for other students? What advice would you give newly bereaved pupils to help them cope with their grief at school?

OLIVIA'S PERSONAL EXPERIENCE

I took my grief and decided that I wasn't going to let it define me; instead, it would be a part of me, but only a part.

For my GCSE English exam, I gave a talk on mental health and suicide which was difficult, but it was a way for me to help heal my pain and anger towards my father. I had people in my class who thought it was odd that I was talking about that because of the connection I had to it, but for me that was a way of reclaiming my love of writing and a way to face the bluntness and truth of my father's death.

I spent time researching facts and statistics, and learning a lot about mental health and suicide, and it was a lot to take on, but it also helped me understand my own grief and loss, too. For me, confronting my cause of bereavement was helpful and healing, but not everyone is ready or wants to focus on the loss, and that's fine. I spent years avoiding talking about my dad's death, and eventually I decided that I was going to be in charge of how I felt about it and I created something meaningful to me, out of the sadness.

Ideas for coping with families

Grief and families

We've talked a lot about getting on with your grief and finding your own way, but *how* you experience your grief will be influenced by others around you, especially those you live with. This might be your family, other relatives or maybe foster carers. This can be a really positive and supportive influence, but it is likely that others are going to be doing their grief differently and at a different speed to you. At times, this can really suck.

If people are stuck in their own grief, they may not be as available to support you through yours. So just when you need some company or to talk something through, maybe your family member can't find a way to be there for you.

> ❝ Tara, whose dad had died, found it really hard to see her mum struggling with so much grief and distress. Sometimes she felt that as well as losing her dad it was as though she had lost her mum too, as just when she needed her mum the most, her mum was absorbed in her own grief and couldn't be there for her.

Equally, sometimes it will be hard to witness the grief of others around you, and you may feel unable to respond to them. This might be because it is already feeling heavy for you, or perhaps you've been having a better day and found it hard to relate at that moment.

Others around you might be 'done' with their grief and focusing on rebuilding their own life. This can leave you feeling quite lonely that they have 'moved on', or angry that they seem to have forgotten the person who died. If they expect you to be done with your grief too, that can add to a sense of isolation. Sometimes it can even make you question whether there is something wrong with you because you're in such a different place. If this is you, we'd like to tell you that there is nothing wrong with you: you're just doing your grief, your way and at your own pace. And that's okay. If this is especially hard for you, make sure you check out the ideas for getting more help in Chapter 3.

It can be helpful to remember that what sometimes appears to be true might not be. People often grieve very privately and to the rest of the world it looks as though they are doing fine. This can mean that while your parent appears to have 'got over it', they may actually be grieving when they are on their own and trying to hold it all together when they are around you, believing that this is protecting you from further upset. Grief can then become the 'elephant in the room' that no one can bear to mention even though it is so clearly right there in the centre of your lives. And by avoiding talking and sharing your experiences of grief, you can all feel disconnected and find it hard to give and receive support from each other.

OLIVIA'S PERSONAL EXPERIENCE

It was often really hard to talk about my dad's death, because not many other people knew him, or what our relationship had been like either, because I had always kept quiet about a lot of it. So, I found it really hard to talk to anyone outside of my mum about everything. But sometimes I found it hard to talk to my mum, too, because she was very angry with him, and I didn't want to tell her I missed him or was sad because I knew she didn't feel the same way and I didn't want to upset her.

And sometimes young people experience grief very much on their own because those they live with maybe didn't know the person who has died. This happens if you end up living with someone who you didn't know very well or at all before your person died. This could be a distant relative or a foster carer, for example. On top of all the challenges that come with grieving, you can find yourself having to get used to living in a new home, with new people, and carrying your grief around. That's a lot. And it can then be hard to really communicate with those you are now living with about the reality of your grief, what it's like for you, what is hard right now and what might help. This doesn't mean that in time you won't all develop good relationships that make you feel more confident to communicate about your grief and feel the benefit of their support.

Other times, young people find themselves carrying their grief on their own in their family if the people they now live with had a poor relationship with the person who died and don't take your grief and feelings of loss seriously. This happened for Liam, whose mum had died from her alcohol addiction:

66 Getting used to living with my dad was hard, and being so far away from my old town and home and school. But probably being away from anyone who cared about my mum was the

hardest. My dad and mum split up because of her drinking and had very little to do with each other after that. When Mum died, Dad acted like he didn't care about her and would always bad-mouth her for having been a drunk.

This made me so mad because I knew the real her. I knew her when she hadn't been drinking and I knew this was the only way she knew how to cope. I was cross that she didn't get more help with her drinking, but, bottom line, she was my mum. It made it really hard to show my feelings about Mum in front of anyone at home as I didn't know how everyone would react and I didn't want to listen to them running her down again.

Families each have their own unique character and way of navigating grief, so as a young person you will be working out what works best for each member of your family as individuals and what works best for you as a family group. With a little bit of work and care for each other, you can often find things that work for everyone, allowing for each other's personal differences but still being able to give each other some support.

OLIVIA'S PERSONAL EXPERIENCE

Sometimes I worry about talking to my younger siblings about Dad because as they get older and more aware of things, they don't necessarily remember or understand what happened. That can feel very lonely, too – not being able to share my grief with those closest to me, and who it affected in a similar way. Just because they're my siblings and we had the same dad doesn't mean that they want to

talk about it, or feel the same way, and that is important
for me to remember when I am talking about it with them.

Grief and other relatives

Other relatives can be an important source of support when
you are grieving. You may have a grandparent, aunt, uncle
or cousin who you can spend time with, so that you can
have a break from the grief at home and benefit from their
support. Relationships with your relatives, however, can also
be complicated at times. As if working out how to navigate
your own grief and that of those you live with wasn't enough,
sometimes these other relationships become more strained,
too. When people are stuck in their own grief, it isn't always
easy for them to notice the needs of others or feel able to
offer empathy or support.

Relationships with relatives can be very special, but they
sometimes become strained for all sorts of reasons after a
death. With emotions running so high and being so raw, it
is not uncommon for there to be lots more stress and distress
between relatives. Some even fall out and lose touch, but this
doesn't necessarily mean forever. If this is happening in your
family, it may feel extra tough for you.

If, for a grandparent, it was their son or daughter who has
died, they may be massively struggling with their own grief,
particularly as parents feel that it is so wrong that children
(even if they are adults) should die before their parents.
And, of course, your aunt or uncle will have lost their
sibling, your parent. Relatives cannot always appreciate
how hard and heavy it is for you to have lost your parent.
Sometimes the circumstances of the death and differences

of opinion about funeral arrangements can put even the strongest of relationships under strain. And with the raw pain of loss, things can be very difficult. This doesn't mean that understanding can't grow and develop over time between everyone.

OLIVIA'S PERSONAL EXPERIENCE

After Dad died, my relationships with relatives from his side of the family were not the same, and I actually don't see them any more. Everyone processes grief differently, and we had different feelings and opinions about Dad and the circumstances in which he died, that unfortunately fractured my relationship with them.

Sometimes it makes me sad that I don't have them in my life, but I also accept that they made their choices and are working through their own grief, too. It wasn't healthy or pleasant for me to be around them, so I stopped trying to force relationships to be 'perfect'. I have family that I can trust and talk to, and that is the most important part of grief and healing: having a healthy support network, not necessarily a big one. I put my grief and healing first for myself, and I am glad that I did because I am important, and I get up each day and choose my life.

Secrets in families

Sometimes there may be information about the person who died that has not been shared with everyone involved. Maybe the adults don't feel able or don't know how to talk to you or your siblings about what happened. In the shock of the death, adults can sometimes feel that telling you that someone important has died and what happened is too much for them, so they withhold some or all of the information. And often they feel that it would be too much for you and want to protect you from further distress. This is hard for you as you might have a sense that you don't know the whole story but feel frustrated that they can't tell you. And it can be hard for the adults fearing that you will find out but still wanting to shield you.

Families might tell older siblings more about what happened and younger ones less. To a degree, this makes sense as younger ones are less likely to understand and take in as many details. But it is important that everyone knows the main parts of the story about the death; otherwise, these secrets can lead to more silence when no one can talk openly or ask questions. This can give you all a harder time supporting each other.

Sometimes the secret started before the death. Maybe your person was ill but you weren't told how ill or that they weren't going to recover. And then they died. Feeling frustrated about this is totally understandable. Feeling completely mad with your family about it is understandable, too. Some young people can turn their feelings on themselves and feel cross with themselves for being stupid and not noticing what was happening. Adults in families don't really do this to deliberately push you out and make it harder for you. It can often be a combination of them not knowing how to tell you and wanting to protect you. Even when someone is very ill and receiving end-of-life care, adults understandably want to hold on to a hope for their recovery; they hope that when it all turns out well, they won't have had to worry you.

In some circumstances, what has happened is known by everyone within the family but a decision is made to keep it *in* the family. Perhaps what happened is something a family fear might lead to bad responses and judgement from others outside. Maybe the circumstances are something that your community or religion have strong beliefs around. This can happen when a death was from suicide or murder, leaving families fearing the judgement of others. In a sense, what happened is none of anyone else's business. But for you, this can make it really hard if you don't have some trusted people to speak to outside your family home and feel that you have to keep the family secret.

As families grieve and find their own ways of coping, they might revisit what they are keeping secret and feel able to share more with you and with others outside the home.

Think it through

Coping with different ways of grieving in your family can be difficult. From the things you have just read, which of those make sense to you and are close to how it's been in your family?

You might want to make a list here (add your own experiences, of course; don't feel limited by what we have suggested):

- . . . .

- . . . .

- ....
- ....
- ....
- ....
- ....
- ....

Of course, grief isn't static; it moves and develops and changes so that things that were hard for a while become less difficult. But sometimes things stay the same because no one has yet found a way to work on them. And for some young people, it might feel like things are getting worse.

Now, have a think about how these things have changed in your family. Does it feel as if things are getting better or worse or staying the same? You could highlight each thing you have listed using a different colour: one colour for getting better, one for getting worse and one for staying the same. Now, how does your list look? Colourful, yes, but is there more of one particular colour? Does this help you understand your own grief a bit more?

Just being able to identify the challenges of grieving within your family can be a helpful step. And realizing they are not uncommon within families as everyone is trying to find their way in difficult circumstances. You will then be in a better position to work out which things you can control and influence to help you manage the challenges that are difficult for you.

Getting on with families

Let's start by thinking about the things that are in your control and things that aren't:

Bring your own ideas to the table here, and maybe add some of ours if they make sense for you.

In my control	Not in my control

Have a look at your list. You will probably find that many of the things that are causing you a lot of stress and distress are not things you can do anything about. That can be frustrating when you realize that you won't necessarily be able to control and change certain things. On the flip side, if you can't control certain things, then you are not responsible for them. That can help you feel a bit lighter.

And now you can use your list of the things you can control

to make your own plan to help you cope with the people around you.

66 For Liam, this helped him to realize that although it was really tough living with people who didn't care about his mum, he couldn't actually control what they did or said. Instead, what he could control was how much influence they had over him. He decided that nothing they could say would change how he felt about his mum, and nothing they could do would stop him grieving for her. He could then control who else he asked for support, and he found that his athletics coach was actually a pretty good listener.

If your family is struggling to talk about their grief, have a think about why this is. Are they in a dark place with their grief and don't even know how to start a conversation? Are you all a bit worried about bringing it up, fearing that you will upset each other? Yes, you may all get upset, but is being upset together something to be afraid of? It might actually be less bad than being upset on your own.

Or are they struggling to talk about their feelings because they are in a different place altogether and your experiences of grief are unique? At some point, you may need to be the one to start a conversation, to get those elephants out of the room so people can communicate. You will probably have ideas about the best way to communicate with those you live with, but here are some ideas that might get you started:

- Mum, can I talk to you for a moment? You don't need to make it all better. I just want to talk to you about how I've been feeling.

- I'm finding it really hard since Jamil died. Can I tell you about it?
- Today was tough because I heard the music that we played at the funeral. What is toughest for you?
- Nan, can you tell me a bit about Mum when she was little? There is so much I still want to know about her. Sometimes, I'm scared that my memory of her is fading.

If communication is really hard, it can result in everyone in your home existing together but each feeling pretty lonely. If you can't talk right now, or others you live with aren't quite up to talking, are there other ways of communicating that don't need words? Have a think about ways of showing them they are important to you. What small gestures can you do that show you care? How can you keep close to them in ways that don't rely on words?

- Making a cup of tea? (If they actually like tea!)
- Doing a household chore without being asked?
- Sending a text to say 'Hi'?
- Giving them a hug?
- Offering to help with or doing the cooking for dinner?
- Finding a movie to watch at home together?

Write your own list of options that fit for you and your relationships with the people you live with.

- . . . .
- . . . .
- . . . .
- . . . .

Be your own buddy

Sometimes young people feel very isolated at home, and you might feel that right now these ideas won't help. We would really like you to give it a go and try something, if you can. It can be really powerful to do a small thing for someone else. It usually helps us even more than the person we do it for.

But if, right now, that's not possible for you, try being your own buddy. When we are in a hard place, we can find that we don't exactly treat ourselves well. We say things to ourselves and even bully ourselves. If this is a bit like you and you're not able to get the close support of others, have a go at being your own best friend. What would a best friend say to you right now? What would they do for you? What advice would they give you that is more helpful than you running yourself down?

Note down a few ideas here:

- ....
- ....
- ....
- ....
- ....

Now store them somewhere – in a cupboard, on your phone, in your diary – so that you can look at them and say them to yourself when you're having a difficult day.

Reforming the family team

As you and those you live with try to cope with your grief as individuals and as a group, you'll get to a stage when you can discover how to work things out together and begin to reform your family team. What we mean draws on an idea of families being like a sports team. Perhaps yours is a doubles team in squash or a five-a-side football team, or maybe your family resembles a full hockey team of 11. Every member of the family has its own position, role and responsibilities. Together you have a history of working out how you all play together best. And then a death happens. Your team is a member down. You all have to work out, often with no notice, how to carry on playing together. And you may have very different ideas about how to do this.

How has your family been readjusting to sharing out roles

and responsibilities? What new positions are you having to play in? How are you covering for each other? And, of course, how are you managing without the person who died? Your team will never be exactly the same again, but it doesn't mean you can't still train together and find a new way of playing together that works out okay for everyone.

We hope some of the ideas in this section help you make sense of what's hard and problem-solve a bit to help with the difficult things about grief and families.

Ideas for coping with further changes in your life

Change is inevitable. Even if no one dies, as you go through life, change happens. It would be pretty dull if everything stayed the same all the time. But sometimes after someone has died – as if that wasn't enough to be coping with – the death can trigger a kind of domino run of more changes and more changes. And along with working out how to cope with your grief, you then find yourself having to adapt again...and again.

Sometimes the changes will have nothing to do with someone dying and would have happened anyway, but on top of your grief, they can feel tough to handle. These include changes that everyone goes through as part of the natural transitions through your teenage years into adulthood – perhaps changes to your external world like leaving school, starting sixth form or even university. And they might be changes to who you are and how you see yourself. People's bodies can change a lot at this stage, and sometimes it can take a while for our thinking to catch up with our bodies and get used to the 'new us'. You might also start to rethink your identity, who you are and how you want others to see you and think about you.

When someone important has died, some people feel that they need everything else to stay the same, so that at least some things feel normal and stable and certain. This is understandable, but it may not be realistic.

OLIVIA'S PERSONAL EXPERIENCE

My world changed in lots of different ways after my dad died. From my parents' working routine, to weekday evenings and weekend activities, everything changed. Family and family friends helped out, so there were more people around, which was also an adjustment. I spent more time with my siblings at my grandparents' house while my mum worked, which changed my routine. Adjustments that change your daily routines can be scary and overwhelming anyway, let alone dealing with those changes as well as the loss of that person.

Talking to my friends and my mum about these changes and how they made me feel helped me adjust to them, and it helped me understand why things had to change. When I was more comfortable with the changes, I realized I could use some of them to help my grief and healing by enjoying the new routines and new things to do.

Different opinions about change

Sometimes after someone has died, people want lots of change, because staying with things how they were is such a reminder of what and who is missing. In families, this can be tricky if some of you want lots of change while others want things to stay the same.

Sometimes families need to pack up the belongings of the person who died really soon for practical reasons. They might need to clear their room or their flat, sell their car or move their belongings. The hospital bed and equipment you had got used to seeing around might be collected really soon. And with it go a mix of memories – not only those that are sad and associated with their illness and treatment but also those last moments you shared.

It can be really painful to lose so many connections with the person who died, especially if it's not what you want. Keeping photos on display or putting them out of sight might be another change that families agree or disagree with. We hope there is a way of compromising so that all of you are listened to and have your views taken into account.

Sometimes families choose to clear out the person's belongings as this is what works for them and helps them focus on their life ahead. Others need to keep things the same way for a while, or sometimes for a very long time. Whatever the pace of change, each probably has its upside and its downside.

Practical changes

As well as physical changes, there may be changes in your daily life in terms of the amount of money your family has and what you're able to do. Perhaps there are activities you enjoyed before that can't be enjoyed right now as there is no one to take you. And even when someone else is able to give you a lift, it doesn't feel the same because you are missing the person who used to watch you play basketball or sing in your choir or go night fishing at the lake.

There may well be lots of changes that no one else notices but are significant to you. Maybe no one does things quite the way your person did. It's not always the practical changes but the ones about the way the home sounds and feels different. Perhaps the way everyone relates to each other just feels really different.

And then there will be the many occasions that will change, including birthdays, celebrations, festivals and anniversaries. Many families develop unique traditions for when and where they open presents, the games they play, the food they eat. Doing this without your person can make their absence really obvious, and this can be really painful. It will probably never feel the same.

Working out what to keep the same as a way of remembering and even honouring the person who died will take some figuring out. Working out what to change to help find new ways of celebrating key events and make new memories will also be important. Working out how to do a bit of both might allow you to both grieve and rebuild your life as in the dual process model, which we talked about in Chapter 1.

RELATIONSHIP CHANGES

When life changes as profoundly as it does when someone important dies, relationships often change, too. This might bring you closer to some people and, at times, make it harder to get on with others, but this doesn't have to be a permanent change.

OLIVIA'S PERSONAL EXPERIENCE

The relationships I have with some family has changed because our grief and memories were different and we didn't share the same thoughts and feelings about my father. That can be hard – the nature of the death can affect more than just your relationship with the person who died – it can affect your relationships with those alive, too. People don't know how they're going to feel or react until they have to grieve and process a death, and unfortunately sometimes relationships change as a result of the death, but it is not your fault and you shouldn't let it affect your grief and healing. These are important to you, and they are things that you can directly impact by making time for them and allowing yourself to heal and feel.

Choice

Let's also think about change and choice. When you have chosen a change, even though it might be hard, it will at least feel a bit easier because it is what you have wanted. And that can help you find a way through. For example, when you choose to join a new club. The change itself might be tough and require a lot of courage and effort when you're grieving, but you can hold on to the fact that it was your decision.

On the other hand, when changes are made for you, it can feel really tough. We hope that if this happened to you, you were at least involved in discussions so that you understand a bit about why a decision has been made.

Some changes are really quite a lot to take in and they may happen immediately after a death. Sometimes when someone dies it can have a knock-on effect when it triggers a whole lot of other changes – like a ripple when a stone hits the water. These might include:

- going to live with a parent you weren't used to living with before
- moving out of your family home
- moving to live with other relatives
- losing contact with some relatives
- moving to live with foster carers
- moving to a new town, or even a new country
- changing to a new school or college, which might also mean travelling in a different way, having to take some different subjects and make new friends
- your parent meeting a new partner
- a new baby in the family.

Make a list of the changes that have happened since your person died.

- . . . .

- . . . .

- ....
- ....
- ....
- ....
- ....
- ....

Now put them on this 'coping line'. Were they easy, okay or really hard to cope with?

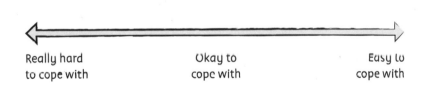

Really hard
to cope with

Okay to
cope with

Easy to
cope with

When change is coming your way

Sometimes anticipating the change is harder than the actual change when it happens. Your mind might get caught up in overthinking all sorts of things about it. But when it happens, you find it wasn't as hard as you had predicted *and* that you coped better than you thought you would. Sometimes we really are stronger than we think.

Some changes can trigger your fears and worries because the change might open up the possibility for something hard to happen again.

" Now that my mum is pregnant again, I can't stop thinking about what happened to my baby brother Jamil who died before he was born. I feel like it is going to happen again to the new baby. So, it is really hard to be excited like everyone around me or even to think about the new baby at all. I usually leave the room when relatives visit and start asking me about names and things. (Kareem)

Getting on with changes

So what can you do to help you cope with the changes that are causing you stress? Sometimes taking a problem-solving approach can help. This sort of approach can help if you have a problem (or problems) that needs solving, or if you have changes that need coping with. This is nothing fancy – in fact, it's very straightforward.

Sometimes if you've got a lot of changes to cope with, or a big problem (or problems) to solve, you feel that you don't know where to start, and you start to feel overwhelmed. And then when you're feeling stressed and overwhelmed like that, it can be difficult to think straight. And then it's difficult to work out what to do, which makes the problems and changes seem even more difficult. If you're not careful you can work yourself up into quite a panic.

But taking a 'systematic' approach to the problems and changes helps you to work things through in a more orderly way. So when your brain is asking you the massive question 'WHAT ARE YOU GOING TO DO ABOUT IT?' instead of replying 'I DON'T KNOW' and then getting more worried, you can say, 'I'm going to follow this problem-solving approach – that's what I'm going to do.'

STEP 1 – MAKE A LIST

Make a list of all the changes that you are having to cope with. Score them from 0–10 to show how much stress they are causing you. You can write this on a piece of paper, make notes on your phone, draw it on a whiteboard – anything you like. But you're going to need to make notes somewhere because there's no way you'll be able to remember everything that you come up with. We want as much brain power as you've got to be thinking about ideas, not trying to remember problems or changes that you've thought of.

STEP 2 – DECIDE WHAT ORDER TO WORK THROUGH THE LIST

Some people like to start with the most stressful change to get that sorted. We like to kind of 'warm up' on a few minor items and then tackle the bigger ones. But you decide where to start.

STEP 3 – CREATE SOLUTIONS AND STRATEGIES FOR EACH ITEM ON YOUR LIST

Come up with lots of ideas. Don't hold back – if you have an idea that seems daft, it goes on the list. And by the way, it doesn't have to be a very neat and ordered actual list – it can be more like a mind map or any other structure that you want to use. If you have an idea that seems impossible, it goes on the list. This is not the time to edit out ideas; this is a time to capture as many ideas as possible. Sometimes the daftest ideas can trigger some very creative and useful ideas.

STEP 4 – STEP AWAY

You don't have to actually physically step away! But before you go through the list of ideas, do something different: go for a walk, make a coffee, watch a video. Anything – just so that your brain gets a break before Step 5.

STEP 5 – ANALYSE

Go through your ideas for each of the problems or changes; cross out the really daft or impossible ones. Then consider the ones that are left – are there one or two that stand out as being good candidates for giving a go? If you can't work out which ones are worth trying, it can be helpful to think about the pros and cons of each one.

STEP 6 – CHOOSE ONE OR TWO

Pick one or two ideas to give a go and make a plan for how to do that.

STEP 7 – DO IT

Do it!

STEP 8 – EVALUATE

A little while after you've put your plan into action, it's a good idea to stop and work out how well it went. Did it help you solve the problem or cope with the change? If it didn't go so well, either try one of the other ideas you came up with or return to Step 3 and come up with some more.

Ideas for moving forwards

When we say 'moving forwards', we're not suggesting that this is 'getting over it'. We're talking about being able to do your grief your way, as well as live your life. You will likely revisit your grief from time to time as you move through your teenage years into adulthood. But moving forwards is important so that you don't feel stuck in your grief. That doesn't mean you're moving forwards all the time. Having bad days, or even longer bad periods is really normal. Having short times when you feel as if you are standing still and things feel really difficult is normal, too. We hope that, overall, you don't feel stuck in your grief all the time. If this does happen a lot, then it would be a good idea to get some additional support, maybe using the ideas in Chapter 3.

Dr Shelley Gilbert's upward spiral of grief that we introduced in Chapter 1 can be helpful to think about moving forward. The spiral can help you to see that although you feel as though you are going round and round, those same feelings usually vary in intensity. Sometimes you feel you are in the heaviest darkest times of sadness and at other times it feels like a much more manageable feeling of sadness and then sometimes just a light shade of sadness. Even when you feel as though you are in the black hole again, you can move outwards and upwards.

Anniversaries

Anniversaries might be really tough – we mean REALLY tough – so don't be surprised, don't be caught out, plan what you can do. You can even plan to be sad at some point, with others or on your own.

Sometimes, the actual date that they died feels really hard as you mark the time – for example, thinking, 'It's one year since they died.' Sometimes, rather than the number date, it is the *day of the week* it happened that is really difficult. If they died on a Sunday morning, each Sunday morning can feel like an anniversary, and when the Sunday closest to the date they died arrives, some young people tell us this is especially hard as the usual Sunday things bring really strong reminders of that particular Sunday. And, of course, significant dates include anniversaries of key moments in the story of what happened – for example, the date they got their diagnosis, the date they moved into the hospice, the last time you saw them. Any or all of these dates can be reminders of really difficult dates.

OLIVIA'S PERSONAL EXPERIENCE

I still struggle with the months before the anniversary of my dad's death. The day itself isn't as hard for me now, but the months leading up to it are because there were factors that ultimately led to his choice and his death.

Certain songs are triggers, and so are some places. I find it easier to avoid these things when the feelings are overwhelming, and over the years I've been able to go back to some of these places, and listen to some of the songs that I used to avoid because I have allowed my grief and time to heal my feelings towards these things.

I also find it hard when I'm sad in the months before the anniversary, because my friends and family know the day Dad died, but it can be hard to explain why I'm sad four months before. But I tell my friends and family, and they understand that grief doesn't just pop back up on the anniversary – it pops up any time it wants to. I just let people know how I feel and that lifts some of the weight, and I talk to people about it, too. The triggers might change, and some might not be triggers forever, but I allow myself to feel all of the emotions, and I don't force myself to get through it or only feel like that on the anniversary.

Maybe your person died a long time ago, or people thought you were too young so didn't tell you the important dates or want to mark them. If you think it would help you to know, think about who in your back-up team could give you this information. But not everyone wants to mark specific dates in their grieving story, and that's okay too.

Being prepared for anniversaries is not about determining that they *will* be really hard but recognizing that they *might* be. You can then prepare yourself for how you might feel and plan for how you might cope. So rather than being really surprised, saying to yourself, 'Oh, this is pretty scary...I'm so upset...why do I feel like this?' instead you say, 'Yep, this feels tough, but feelings pass and so will this one. I'm going to lean into my feelings and try to see what helps.'

Young people sometimes tell us that the run-up to the anniversary can be the trickiest time. They put lots of effort into imagining how they might feel, and then when the day comes, it's hard, but they cope. Sometimes they even benefit from marking the date by doing something special to remember the person and help them feel close to them. They might want to visit the grave or somewhere where their ashes were buried or scattered. But they also find it helpful to try to do something special that their person enjoyed doing, eating their favourite food, meeting up with others who cared about them and you.

One thing we think is important is to be around people and not to spend too much time on your own on difficult days. That doesn't mean that maybe having a bit of time to yourself isn't important for you, but when days are hard and we find ourselves struggling, extra support is needed. Often that can come from the people we live with. If you are all grieving for your special person, then maybe you can support each other and find things that bring you close. If that is not possible, then think about who else in your support team would be good to be around.

66 Dylan was dreading the anniversary of their mum's death and wasn't sure how they would cope as they didn't think their foster parents would understand. When their foster parents told them of the weekend plans, they said that they didn't really want to go to a family barbecue as it will be the anniversary of their mum dying.

Once their foster parents understood, they talked with Dylan about what they would like to do. They really wanted to go to the grave. This would be the first time. They all made a plan for taking a trip to Dylan's hometown and going to the cemetery where they had some time alone at their mum's grave. Although this was hard, they also got a sense of comfort from being there. And their foster parents saw how important this was.

Of course, not all difficult dates are to do with your person dying. Their birthday, your birthday and other important calendar events can also bring back painful memories and a new wave of grief at not having them in your life. Sometimes there will be something that was personal to you both that is another loss. Maybe you always watched the cup final or the final of a TV talent show together, so when that comes round each year, you find that was an anniversary you perhaps didn't expect.

Predict, permit, plan

Judith Cohen, a psychologist who works with bereaved young people, has found that the following can be helpful:

- **Predict** – try to think ahead and work out when you might find things difficult, perhaps based on previous times you've found hard.
- **Plan** – work out what things will help you get through the day and who could support you with this.
- **Permit** – give yourself permission to feel whatever strong feelings the day brings. It's okay. Like Shelley Gilbert's spiral, it doesn't mean you'll stay in a black hole of grief.

Have a go.

PREDICT

Write a list of times that you predict will be more tricky (you might have already faced some difficult times so know from experience).

1. . . . .

2. . . . .

3. . . . .

4. . . . .

5. . . . .

PLAN

Write down ideas for things to do that day to help you get through it. You might add in who you want to spend time with you for support.

1. . . . .

2. . . . .

3. . . . .

4. . . . .

5. . . . .

PERMIT

Write a list of how you think these days will make you feel.

1. . . . .

2. . . . .

3. . . . .

4. . . . .

5. . . . .

And then write down something you will tell yourself, giving yourself permission to have these feelings and not feel bad about having them.

I'll say to myself:

. . . .

. . . .

. . . .

Maybe things won't be as difficult as you predicted, but having a plan can give you security that you've got ideas, things to tell yourself and people to help.

Learning to recognize and understand how you are doing is really important as you move forward. You may be affected by different things and in different ways, but knowing when you're doing okay, and noticing when you're not, can help you.

Maybe you'll start to have problems with sleeping or eating, or learning, or finding the motivation to do things you usually enjoy. Knowing how grief and stress affects you can help you keep safe. And if you've noticed that you're not doing so well, be prepared to speak with someone who can help you get the support you need. (There are some ideas in Chapter 3.)

Growing your world

In Chapter 1, we introduced Lois Tonkin's idea about growing around your grief, where rather than your grief getting smaller over time, you learn to 'grow your world' so that it kind of offsets how much your grief hurts.

Think about ways in which you have been 'growing around your grief' by doing things, trying things, having a go at making your life a bit more fulfilling, even if it's only in small ways. Each small effort really can build up to help with this.

Kareem was surprised when he started thinking about how he was growing around his grief:

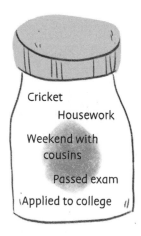

Cricket
Housework
Weekend with cousins
Passed exam
Applied to college

What would your jar look like? What size is your jar and your grief within it? And what could you add to encourage yourself about how you are doing at growing your world?

Maybe add your ideas here:

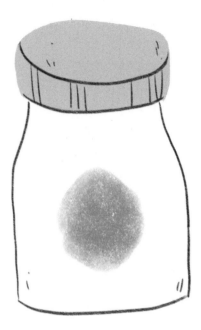

It can be difficult to realize how far you have come when you're caught up in your grief in daily life. But spending a moment and giving it a bit of attention can encourage you that you're doing okay. And if you feel that this activity actually shows you that it's not been so easy to grow your world, try this:

1. Do some focused thinking and set just one small (it can be *really* small) goal of something you think you could try that would feel like a step forward.
2. Work out who in your support team could help with this.
3. Set yourself a timeframe to work on that one thing over one week. Or is a fortnight more realistic?

4. Then check in with yourself to see how you have done.

5. If you have managed that one thing, give yourself a large pat on the back (if that really isn't satisfying, you can choose a better reward!). And then go back to Step 1 and set another goal to keep the momentum going. Growing around your grief isn't a one-off thing.

6. If you found that you didn't achieve the first goal, then think through why that was. Was it because of any of these?

   - The goal was too big for a first goal.
   - You weren't ready for it.
   - Practical things got in the way of doing it (e.g. you couldn't get a lift).
   - You forgot all about it!

Or was there a different reason? Now you've worked out the reason, can you problem-solve to work out the next step to help with this?

Growing around your grief is a powerful way of showing yourself that you are moving forwards. Although the death of your person will most likely have shaped you (maybe just a bit or maybe a whole lot) because it is such a significant event, it doesn't have to define you and be the only thing about you. You are more than your grief.

Holding on to hope

Another thing that young people have told us is helpful is finding something to be hopeful about. This doesn't mean that you have to let go of your pain or your memories of the person who died (unless it would help to). But finding something to hope for can bring some balance to your difficult experiences.

If feeling hopeful right now feels the total opposite of what you are feeling, then maybe press pause on this idea and come back to it in a while. Or maybe ask someone in your support team to remind you of what you used to be hopeful about. And they can hold on to that hope for you. It's kind of like not throwing out everything just because it's so hard for you right now. The future doesn't have to be as heavy as the present.

66 Dylan found that they couldn't imagine going back to band practice ever, EVER, EVER again. They were ready to throw out their guitar and all the music they had been writing with the band. But even though they were feeling like giving up, their band mates said they weren't giving up and that although Dylan couldn't make it to band practice right now, they would keep practising and be waiting when they were ready. That was so important for Dylan to hear.

Final words

Grieving can be tough, and there aren't really any shortcuts. We hope that this book has helped you to understand what's going on and has given you some ideas for how to cope with it. The fact that you bothered to pick up this book says something about your motivation to do something about what you are going through. Hang on in there.

Chapter 3

GETTING SPECIALIST HELP

We hope you've already realized that you don't need to be doing this on your own, and that you can lean on family, friends or other folk who can support you such as teachers, youth club leaders, neighbours. And we hope that reading this book will also have helped. But sometimes it can be really helpful to get a little additional help from an expert. Here are some signs that mean you might want to get a bit of expert support:

- Feelings are really intense all of the time.
- Difficulties and distress going on and on for ages.
- Getting steadily worse (things tend to go up and down anyway; here, we're talking about a steady decline).
- Feeling hopeless.
- Making you feel like you don't want to be alive.

In the next section, we've listed some ideas of where you might get some extra help. You might want to share this with an adult who can help you get the additional support.

Useful places to get more information

At a Loss (www.ataloss.org) can help you or someone looking after you find a specialist bereavement service, or additional resources.

Child Bereavement UK (www.childbereavementuk.org) is a child bereavement charity that also offers a free helpline (0800 02 888 40) and chat services, as well as providing direct support to bereaved children and young people in some areas of the UK.

Childline (www.childline.org.uk) is a free and confidential helpline for young people in the UK – online, on the phone, any time. Call 0800 11 11 or contact them online through their website.

Cruse (www.cruse.org.uk/get-support/supporting-children-and-young-people) is a nationwide bereavement support service to help people through the most painful experience of their life. They have a network of volunteers who offer 1:1 support to children and young people.

Grief Encounter (www.griefencounter.org.uk) supports children and young people nationally, including their helpline (0808 802 0111), email and chat, 1-1 and group counselling. Their specialist resources include *Grief Book* and *Mr Good Grief*. Direct support is provided from their centres in Mill Hill (North London) and Bristol.

Hope Again (www.hopeagain.org.uk) is a website from Cruse Bereavement Support specifically for young people who are bereaved. There are lots of resources, including a short film called *Hope in Grief* where young people tell a little bit about their story, how their bereavement has affected them and what helps them get through.

Papyrus (www.papyrus-uk.org/aboutus) is a charity dedicated to the prevention of young suicide. If you are experiencing thoughts of suicide, you can contact them from 9 a.m. until midnight every day of the year by phone (0800 068 4141), text (07860 039967) and email (pat@papyrus-uk.org).

Samaritans (www.samaritans.org) is a charity that provides support to anyone struggling with their emotions. You can contact them by phone (116 123) at any time day or night, or you can use email (jo@samaritans.org).

Winston's Wish (www.winstonswish.org) is a child bereavement charity that offers a helpline (08088 020 021), and you can also contact them by email or by chat via the website. They also have some resources that might be useful.

In your school, there may be posters with helpline telephone numbers – many of these will be able to provide some immediate support if you need someone to talk to.

Getting support in a group can sound like the scariest possible thing, but often it can be the most powerful thing to meet with others who are grieving. These are the people who are most likely to understand what you are going through. Often you have to be brave to go somewhere new and meet new people and think about your grief. But hey, you've been doing many brave things adapting to new changes and challenges, so don't rule it out. Maybe ask for some information to help you understand what will happen at the group.

APPENDIX

THE PHYSICAL COST

	Not at all	A bit	A lot
I am more tired	☐	☐	☐
It's hard to get to sleep or stay asleep	☐	☐	☐
I haven't got much energy	☐	☐	☐
My body feels in shock	☐	☐	☐
My body feels heavy and sluggish	☐	☐	☐
My chest (or heart) feels heavy	☐	☐	☐
My body feels restless so it's hard to relax	☐	☐	☐
My throat feels tight or as though there's a knot in it	☐	☐	☐
My eyes feel like they could cry at any moment	☐	☐	☐
My head is a bit foggy and confused	☐	☐	☐
My stomach has a knot in it or just won't settle	☐	☐	☐
It is harder to eat	☐	☐	☐
I keep wanting to eat	☐	☐	☐
(Write in your own)	☐	☐	☐
. . . .			
(Write in your own)	☐	☐	☐
. . . .			

THE EMOTIONAL COST

	Not at all	A bit	A lot
I feel sad or upset	☐	☐	☐
I feel worried or scared	☐	☐	☐
I feel cross or annoyed	☐	☐	☐
I feel guilty or ashamed	☐	☐	☐
I feel lonely	☐	☐	☐
I feel heartbroken	☐	☐	☐
My feelings change a lot	☐	☐	☐
My feelings get in the way of doing stuff	☐	☐	☐
I get opposite feelings that are tricky to manage (e.g. sad and happy at the same time)	☐	☐	☐
My feelings are so big that they overwhelm me	☐	☐	☐
(Write in your own)	☐	☐	☐
. . . .			
(Write in your own)	☐	☐	☐
. . . .			

THE THINKING COST

	Not at all	A bit	A lot
It's hard to concentrate	☐	☐	☐
I keep forgetting things	☐	☐	☐
I feel like I'm in a fog	☐	☐	☐
My mind keeps thinking about what happened	☐	☐	☐
I keep trying to make sense of something that doesn't really make sense	☐	☐	☐
I spend a lot of time trying NOT to think about what happened	☐	☐	☐
I'm thinking about me and my life in an unhelpful way	☐	☐	☐
I'm thinking about other people in an unhelpful way	☐	☐	☐
I'm thinking about the world around me in an unhelpful way	☐	☐	☐
(Write in your own)	☐	☐	☐
. . . .			
(Write in your own)	☐	☐	☐
. . . .			

THE PRACTICAL COST

	Not at all	A bit	A lot
My morning has changed	☐	☐	☐
My daytime has changed	☐	☐	☐
My evening has changed	☐	☐	☐
My weekends have changed	☐	☐	☐
Who I get to see has changed	☐	☐	☐
Who I live with has changed	☐	☐	☐
Where I go to school has changed	☐	☐	☐
Things I used to enjoy have stopped	☐	☐	☐
My responsibilities have changed	☐	☐	☐
The people I used to rely on have changed	☐	☐	☐
(Write in your own)	☐	☐	☐
. . . .			
(Write in your own)	☐	☐	☐
. . . .			

The authors

Beck

Olivia

David